30
Miles
for
Ice Cream

30 Miles for Ice Cream

Murray Hoyt

Illustrations by Aldren A. Watson

The Stephen Greene Press

BRATTLEBORO, VERMONT

This book has been produced in the United States of America: designed by
Aldren A. Watson, composed, printed, and bound by The Colonial Press.
It is published by The Stephen Greene Press,
Brattleboro, Vermont 05301.

Library of Congress Cataloging in Publication Data
Hoyt, Murray.
    30 miles for ice cream.

    Autobiographical.
    1. Country life—Vermont.   2. Hoyt, Murray.
I. Title.
S521.5.V5H693   917.43 5 [B]   74–13101
ISBN 0–8289–0230–5   *HoyT*

74 75 76 77 78 79 9 8 7 6 5 4 3 2 1

Contents

Whatever Did You Do, Mr. Hoyt?   *ix*

1
That's the Way It Was   *1*

2
It's Never Tasted Better   *8*

3
"The Wind She Blow on Lac Champlain"   *19*

4
Total War with an Outboard Motor   *34*

5
Fishing for Food and Fun   *47*

6
Living Off the Land   *62*

7
Bee Hunting   *74*

8
The Visit of Troop 24   *85*

9
What We Did Instead   *96*

10
Winter on Lake Champlain   *110*

11
Cliff-top and College   *132*

12
By No Means Big League   *142*

13
Hunting Ducks   *159*

14
What—A Turkey Hunt in a Vermont Barn?   *175*

15
Then and Now   *183*

Whatever Did You Do, Mr. Hoyt?

A sweet young thing in her late teens said to me last summer, "Mr. Hoyt, you must remember 'way, 'way back when there was just nothing interesting going on in the world: no outer-space program, no television, no radio even, no cars, no fast boats or water skiing, no tractors, no movies, no running water, no plumbing. Just *nothing*."

"Would you believe," I asked her, "that George Washington and I used to commiserate with each other about that very situation?"

And she said, "Oh, *you!* But seriously, whatever did people *do?* How did they get around? Especially 'way up here in Vermont away from everywhere? And with nobody earning much money?"

I went home and thought about this a lot. Several generations have come along whose members have no firsthand knowledge of what life with low earnings and without modern inventions was like. They feel sorry for us, probably rightly, for having been born too soon.

So this is my attempt to show them how awful it really was. . . .

1

That's the Way It Was

Beginning when I was two years old, I spent my summers with my family on Lake Champlain in our cottage on Potash Bay. Potash Bay is in West Addison, which in turn is about two-thirds of the way north in Vermont. Today there are two dozen cottages along the shores of the bay, but at that time ours, which we called "Cliff-top," was the only one. It was set on corner rocks and was made of novelty siding on studding. There was no road to it; we had to reach it through a gate and along the edge of a hayfield. The gate had to be kept closed for fear cows might get into the meadow and trample the hay. The trip through the hayfield was about a quarter of a mile.

The cottage had a huge screened porch on which my parents and I did most of our living and where we slept at night. There was a large living room with fireplace, a tiny kitchen, and, upstairs, four bedrooms. The plumbing wasn't. Its place was taken by a small building known by the somewhat less-than-frank title of "woodshed." Lake water was forced up into a storage tank on the second floor by a one-manpower pump, and from there reached a single faucet in the kitchen below by gravity. Any hot water was heated in a teakettle on the kitchen range or oil stove.

Similar cottages along Potash Bay today are sold at a figure between ten thousand and twenty thousand dollars. In 1907 my parents had spent the then magnificent sum of $1000 to erect these buildings.

I thought, very simply, that it was paradise. My father, Prentiss Hoyt, had been born and spent his boyhood near that cottage, but by the time I speak of he was the head of the English Department at Clark University. Therefore we lived in Worcester, Massachusetts, during the school year.

For weeks before our leaving Worcester for the summer I planned and dreamed of the camp and the lake, and I'd pack fishing tackle and other things that mattered, days in advance of our scheduled departure.

We got up very early on the chosen morning, and rode on a trolley to Union Depot, where we boarded the train for Winchendon. At Winchendon we changed to the Boston section of the rather optimistically named *Green Mountain Flyer.*

My father always found two green plush-cushioned seats together and turned over the back of one so that we could sit together. The hours dragged, but were helped in their passing by trips to the water cooler in the end of the coach, and by the visits of the "news butcher," a uniformed man who came through with papers, magazines, books, candy, fruit, and gum for sale. He would occasionally give out little squares of milk chocolate, handled delicately with a small pair of tongs, as a sample of his wares. And at other times he would leave a magazine on the seat and collect it or the money on his next trip through.

I was allowed to eat the samples, but not to touch the magazines or buy the chocolate because the price was a whole nickel higher than the price would be at a store. The large box lunch which my mother had put up, we ate at noon; this helped pass the time. There was a diner, but the prices charged were "outrageous, actually sometimes as much as *two whole dollars* for just a dinner," and the box lunch was our answer. We finally reached Vergennes, Vermont, in midafternoon.

Here we were met by a farmer with a pair of horses and a double wagon. We bought a long list of groceries at Dalrymple's Store, sometimes as much as five dollars' worth, but of course some of those staples would last all summer. These groceries we loaded into the wagon, and we started our ten-mile ride to the lake. It was slow going. The horses trotted some on the level, but walked far too much to suit me; we moved at about four miles an hour. When we reached the watering trough on Creamery Hill in Addison, the driver got out and loosened the checkrein and the horses drank.

These were Morgans, and would be hitched to a hayrack to pull huge loads of hay the next day. But before that day's work started, my father and I would go up to the farmer's barn where our boat had been kept during the winter, help load it onto the hayrack and drive it to the lake. There the horses would back the wagon a bumpy, scary distance out into the water, and we would slide the boat off until it floated, and row it to our beach.

Those first nights were always so still it was hard to sleep out there on the screened porch. No sound of trolleys, no noises of those new contraptions called automobiles. The splash of a fish feeding late, perhaps. Sometimes there'd be the imbecile laugh of a loon, or the squawk of a heron or, if the wind was right, the sound of sheep or cows in a distant pasture.

We always took a quick dip in the lake before we dressed in the morning. We did this raw. Even when we had guests, that was the procedure. And my parents had a lot of guests, just as anyone living next to a lake always does; sometimes all four rooms upstairs were full. There was a lot of gaiety and laughter and give-and-take because these people didn't seem to realize there was nothing to do. The bathing area couldn't be seen down over the cliff from the cottage and the women were supposed to go down in bathrobes, and when they had all returned the men all went down in bathrobes. We laid these aside and we swam in the all-together. And nobody was supposed to peek, and to the best of my knowledge nobody ever did; nor were there boats or cottages to overlook the spot. Thus we kept our bathing suits dry for the before-dinner swim.

We fished every morning except Sundays. My father bought milk at a farm a mile away by water—five cents a quart—and we'd troll over and back using long bamboo-pole outriggers. My father always said it gave him a perfect excuse to fish regularly.

We did very well with the fishing. We ate fish nearly every day for two reasons: it was good, and meat was hard for us to buy or to keep fresh. We had to walk about five miles to the nearest grocery store by land, but by water we could row about four miles to stores in Port Henry, New York, across the lake. So we didn't do much tripping to the store for meat. In addition to the northern pike that we caught trolling, we still-fished for perch, sheepshead, bass and other varieties, in the late afternoons.

There was one meat cart which came around once each week. If you phoned them the day before, they'd bring along any groceries you wanted them to bring. But since we had to walk up and meet the cart at the road, and also because telephoning was such an emotional experience, we used this service sparingly.

Telephoning. Now there was something. You walked up to the nearest farmhouse that had a phone and you picked up the receiver from a hook on the side of the wooden box on the wall. The mouthpiece stuck out at you on a metal arm. You heard all sorts of ghost voices; it was nearly impossible to tell whether one set was loud enough to mean your own line was being used or not.

If you thought it wasn't, you held down the receiver and cranked the crank on the side of the box the requisite number of longs and shorts to get the party you were after. Then there was a lot of shouting. The voice you heard wasn't much louder than the other ghost voices, and there was much "What?—*what?*—louder, I can't hear you." Usually you were able to get your message across; sometimes you weren't and the farmer's wife graciously agreed to call later and relay the message when the telephone was less noisy. Or when less people were listening-in to cut down the volume. Listening-in every time the phone rang was a way of life in the country.

One bachelor farmer used to sit near his telephone in the evenings and add a long ring to whatever came through. This would get a wrong party, and when that mistake had been cleared up and the ring came through again, this time he'd add a short ring with his crank. Another wait. Then the number again, and this time he'd add two shorts. He successfully kept evening phone service in that area at a minimum for years.

About once a week there'd be a "sociable" at the Community House. Or there'd be a church-sponsored "entertainment" to raise money for the Ladies Aid. My father gave readings, and my mother was a trained musician, so the church would be anxious enough for us to perform to have someone stop for us with a horse and carriage. The ice cream at these functions was yellow and smooth from the heavy rich cream used, and it had been made in an ice-cream freezer the handle of which had been turned by hand, while salt and last winter's lake ice from an icehouse were packed in around the whirling container with its dasher turning inside. It was a kid's job to lick the dasher when it was removed from the finished product, a delightful chore.

Most evenings we read by kerosene lamps and went to bed early, sleepy from the sun and the swimming and the exercise. We got up early each morning. On Sundays and on rainy days there were a lot of rowboats trolling. The farmers had no cars and town was a long way away. So they fished on rainy days. They never fish now.

On good days, in haying season, some farmer friend would get caught with a lot of hay down and come and ask my father if he'd help by pitching hay the next day. My father would, and I would be allowed to ride on the load of hay and drive the horses from one haycock to the next. And to tread down the wonderful-smelling hay in the mow as it was being pitched off. There would be a huge meal of fricasseed chicken at noon, and between loads the farmer and my father and I would drink an iced thirst-quencher made of water with ginger in it. This was considered more effective on a hot day than plain water.

Except for boats that rowed past on Sundays and rainy days, we'd see no one, week in and week out, except those who came to see us. The side-wheel steamer *Vermont* would go by about eleven o'clock each day on its trip from Plattsburgh, New York, to Ticonderoga and return, and we knew exactly how many minutes it would be before her wake would have crossed a couple of miles of water and would crash against our shore. Once in a while the steamer *Ticonderoga* would come down on a moonlight excursion, dock at Loomis's dock two miles above us and unload apple barrels. We'd see her lights round Barber's Point near Westport, and we'd row up to Loomis's dock and sit in the dark in our skiff and watch the excitement and the running stevedores with their small-wheeled dollies. There was often an orchestra playing for dancing on the afterdeck. It was very gay.

Once each summer there'd be an excursion from Port Henry and we'd row over and go on it. When the

"Ti" returned to port she'd blow the contents of her firebox. Huge jets of live coals would shoot out from her side and hiss into the water. Afterward we'd row home in the night, and the Delaware & Hudson train sliding along its track close to the water on the York State side would look like a lighted snake. It was an amazing feeling to a small boy to watch it and wonder who were on it and where they were going.

We'd take the skiff and go along the beach collecting driftwood for our fireplace; there were no houses and the windrow of wood deposited by spring's high water was for the taking. We'd set up sideboards and pile the wood higher than our heads as we sat amidships to row home.

We'd gather wild strawberries for shortcake, later wild raspberries and blackberries. We'd hunt bees on a pleasant afternoon. Now and then we'd have to walk to where the cream wagon, which collected cream from the farms for the creamery in Addison, was kept at night. On a certain day each week creamery butter was left in one of the containers for us.

Once we paddled to Vergennes, up Otter Creek, to get an ice-cream sundae, a round-trip distance of thirty-odd miles for the day. We went on picnics by boat or canoe. On the Fourth of July we always rowed out into the lake after dark far enough so that we could watch the fireworks display at Port Henry and at Westport and Basin Harbor, all at the same time. Coming home from still-fishing across the bay after dark, sometimes my mother would sing if the night was still. As the summer drew to a close and our remaining days became few, I'd sit up in the bow where nobody could see me plainly, and maybe shed a silent tear or two because I wanted so badly to stay longer in that lovely place. I remember this poignantly.

All too soon would come the last day, and the hayrack to pick up the boat, over where the road dipped down next to the lake. Last of all we put on the blinds.

And then the horses and the wagon would come to take us to Vergennes and the train, and the train to take us back to Worcester.

The groceries for the whole summer cost less than twenty dollars, and if it hadn't been for all the entertaining, would have been far less even than that.

As I think back on it, there must have been something wrong with me not to need a car or a motorcycle or a speedboat or a radio or a television set or lots of money. But even though it shows me as being a person who didn't know enough to miss the good and interesting things in life, anyway that's how it was.

2

It's Never Tasted Better

I think the area in which everyone feels sorriest for us old gaffers and gafferesses who lived before anything worthwhile had been discovered or invented, is in transportation. Either we were stuck in one place all our lives, or if we were able to get away a few miles it took forever to do it.

Looking back from the vantage point of today's transportation marvels it *was* bad. Endless days were spent just in traveling short distances. Much energy was used up in walking. Why believe it or not—now hold on to your hats—in those days golfers used to have to *walk* around the golf courses of our land. And skiers used to have to climb up a hill before they could slide down it.

Fortunately most of us didn't even realize how bad off we were. That made it bearable, I guess. That thirty-odd-mile-round-trip paddle by canoe for an ice-cream sundae that I mentioned, is a case in point. Everybody in the area knows that nowadays you could hop into your car and drive to Vergennes from our Lake Champlain camp in fifteen or twenty minutes, eat your sundae if you could find a place to buy one, and drive home without losing even an hour. Yet the trip by water took us all day. Let me tell you how it went.

For days ahead of the chosen day we were excited about the trip. "We" meant Sidney Gage, my buddy from Worcester who was visiting me, and me. And to a certain extent my father, who was to take the trip with us.

We woke very early. We packed the noon lunch in the canoe, the extra paddles, jackets, rain gear. The fact that we didn't take bathing suits had nothing to do with our plans for an occasional cooling swim. Another thing we didn't take was drinking water. Why should we? Weren't we passing over mile after mile of sparklingly clear blue water, purer than any reservoir anywhere?

We took fifteen-minute shifts at paddling. My father paddled in the stern, the command post of a canoe, and I paddled bow for fifteen minutes and Sid paddled bow for the next fifteen. Then I paddled, then he paddled. At the end of the first hour, I took over the stern seat from my father and he rested for fifteen minutes while Sid and I both paddled. During the days before the start my father had made us practice, over shallow water, the correct way to change places in a canoe. He felt that this was necessary even with a wide and relatively stable canoe like ours.

We made splendid time, just over three miles an hour. The day was bright and beautiful with little or no wind. The birds, the boats, the people on shore were all extremely interesting. Now and then we'd see a school of perch "riffling," driving schools of minnows to the surface and decimating them.

The person resting in the middle of the canoe would

man the field glasses and examine the expanse of water or shore and tell the other two of us about the things he was able to see with them that we couldn't. The field glasses were, incidentally, tied to a stay in the canoe so that, if there *should* be an accident, they would not be lost.

Lake Champlain is a 120-mile, north-south waterway over which have traveled, from long before white men first came to this continent, an incredible number of people and an incredible volume of goods. Indian war canoes, smaller canoes, bateaux, rowboats, skiffs, thousands of sailboats, all plied its waters. Then came tugboats, towboats, passenger and freight steamers, launches, and finally, in our time, oil barges, paper barges and speedboats.

Whole fleets of naval vessels appeared on its surface, and disappeared again. Forts were built which commanded its narrowest points, were garrisoned for some years, then abandoned to the decay of wood and the crumbling of mortar. The course of North America's history was vastly influenced by happenings upon its waters and upon its shores. In the early days particularly, when wilderness was everywhere, everything that moved swiftly had to be funneled along this great waterway.

Because this was so, you couldn't proceed very far over Champlain waters without coming upon some interesting place, or some spot where a significant historic event had taken place. And in our family, at least, my father, who was a good storyteller, could and did make these events live in such a way that they captured the imagination of a young boy and his buddy. I would, for a few moments, feel as if I were paddling a war canoe instead of an Old Town, or was aboard a warship under sail trying to escape British pursuit, or was in some other way a part of whatever event my father was describing.

On our journey for ice cream that day we came first

to Mud Island, where my father had once watched a family of otters slide down the clay bank, then climb up to do it over and over again. The water on their fur kept the clay slide slick and fast, and for as long as my father watched they continued to have the sort of hilarious family party which is hard for human beings to believe that animals ever have. While we were passing Mud Island he told us what he had seen.

On to the north we reached Arnold's Bay, a small, almost landlocked basin. My father had told us on other occasions what had happened there to give it that name.

After the naval battle at Valcour Island in 1776, Benedict Arnold with some of the remnants of the American fleet fled south pursued by the British. When he reached that small bay he set fire to his ships and burned them to the waterline, then fled farther south by land. It was rumored that waterlogged timbers from the bottoms of these ships could still be seen if the water was very clear the day you looked.

We began to drift slowly back and forth inside Arnold's Bay, all three of us trying to look past the sheen on the water and into its depths. We saw a lot of shadows that might have been timbers, but we never knew whether or not they actually were.

We started on. With the glasses we could see the buildings of Camp Dudley, the New York City Y.M.C.A. camp on the New York shore, the oldest boys' camp in the United States. The waterfront was busy at that time in the morning.

Now and then one of us would get thirsty. When he did he would lift his paddle from the water, hold it slantwise above him so that the water running down from the paddle blade would run into his open mouth. If the flow lessened, he immersed the blade in the water and lifted it again. It would amaze you how simple this method was, how quick, and how satisfactory.

We paddled across the mouth of Button Bay, which

sometimes on maps is called Button Mold Bay. It's name was derived from the fact that along its shores could be found a great many "buttons" of hardened clay. Many of these were perfect with two, three, or four threadholes. The clay in that bay hardened around the stems of grass and weeds which had, through the years, rotted and left the round, flat, hard clay buttons with holes that were like threadholes. We went ashore and picked up a few handfuls of perfect ones.

There is a pile of rocks off the tip of the next point which is called Scotch Bonnet. We eased the canoe in there to take a short swim; by then the day was beginning to grow quite warm. The water was very clear and the swim was particularly satisfying because in spots you could dive right off the rocks into deep water.

We approached Kellogg's Bay and, just beyond it, Otter Creek's mouth. Kellogg's Bay is very shallow, made so by silt brought down by the river.

Through the centuries the Otter has built for itself two narrow fingers of land, one on each side of the channel, extending well out into the lake. As we approached the channel my father told us that in the late 1750's Major Robert Rogers had led an expedition of canoes and bateaux north from Fort Crown Point against the St. Francis Indians in Canada. The French, however, had set up a blockade of the lake. And they had set it up across the narrowed lake from those slender fingers of land and Split Rock Mountain on the New York shore.

Rogers and his men, under cover of darkness, kept close to shore in the very shallow Kellogg's Bay where there was only a foot or two of water. This was enough to float the canoes and bateaux. It never occurred to the French that anyone could travel in such shallow water.

They moved very silently until they came to the base of the first finger of land. They disembarked, slid the canoes and bateaux across the landspit and into the river, then embarked again and crossed the river.

They crossed the finger of land on the other side in the same way, re-embarked, kept close to the shore of *that* bay, and continued on up the lake. The French never knew their line of blockading warships had been bypassed.

As we approached the Otter and the long fingers of land, we could see exactly how the plan would have worked. It gave you a funny feeling to be passing in a modern canoe the very place where this event had taken place many years before, with those other canoes.

Many years after Sid and my father and I took this trip, a movie was made of this historical incident, starring Spencer Tracy. But Hollywood, as is its custom, hammed it up considerably. The two fingers of land are actually very narrow and only a few feet above water level. Yet the movie had the men dragging those boats up a young mountain and letting them down the other side. A prodigious effort.

Once we were in Otter Creek, the water was glasslike. The lake's surface had been wrinkled by a breeze; there was no breeze in the tree-lined river. You could see two images, the scene along the bank as it actually was, and the upside-down reflected scene; one was as clear as the other. Behind us, though, the reflected scene was broken up by the slight commotion of our passing. It was very beautiful, like some tropical river.

We had progressed a short distance and I was in the bow. Everything was quiet in the extreme.

I reached my paddle forward to take the next stroke—and when the paddle was a couple of inches away from the water, the water exploded under it.

I mean actually exploded. Spray cascaded onto me. I lurched violently and my father in the stern had to do some quick balancing to keep the canoe upright.

I almost fell apart; I took it big. I was literally startled out of my wits. For a few seconds, I didn't think: I felt and reacted. Imagine, if you can, how you would

13

have felt if the world around you were placid and quiet, no one anywhere near, and suddenly there came a great splash right beside you.

Sid laughed. My father was more adroit at hiding his feelings, but you could see that he was much amused. I was hopping mad.

First I accused them of doing whatever had been done. They denied this of course and patiently convinced me they were blameless. Then I wanted to know what *had* happened. Nobody knew for sure. My father guessed it was some sort of fish, and this seemed likely. The others had been startled too, but they hadn't been as close to the area where the bomb had burst as I was.

"He was probably sunning himself, saw your paddle about to come down on him, and went somewhere else."

My fur was still ruffled and that "went somewhere else" struck me as being the understatement of the year.

I let out a heartfelt and indignant "Hah!"

We began to paddle again, but the paddling on my part was very gingerly. I looked at the water searchingly each time I was about to put my paddle into it.

It had been close to the end of my fifteen minutes, and Sid and I traded places when the proper time came. I was still being a little stiff toward Sid because he had laughed at me. The canoe moved forward again with Sid in the bow seat.

Suddenly the water exploded close to him and *he* nearly tipped us over. Water was splashed on *him*. He took it as big as I had, and in addition dropped his paddle.

I was startled too, but even such a short extra distance between me and the explosion cut 'way down on its effect. I recovered instantly and I laughed nastily. After that I felt better.

We started on with Sid paddling just as gingerly as I had, being just as careful each time he brought his paddle forward.

15

This time we looked on all sides of the boat, and very shortly we saw something that looked like a small log about fifteen feet away and just under the surface. Moments later we saw one about ten feet off, and this one moved slowly farther away. My father made a quick motion at it with his paddle, and it accelerated.

"I saw that one then," he said. "It was a billfish."

I have looked the species up since, and what we locally used to call a billfish because of the long wicked-toothed bill used for a mouth, is correctly known as a gar. It is long and thin—one side or the other of three feet—brownish in color, and looks like an emaciated swordfish except that the swordfish has only the upper part of its bill. The gar has both an upper and lower part. A gar of course is awfully small in comparison to a swordfish, but still is awfully big for a freshwater fish. And I had just discovered the hard way that he rates "A" for agility when a canoe bears down on him swiftly while he's dozing.

I had seen billfish a few times on still, sunny days while we were trolling, but never in such quantity as this. My father on such occasions had always reacted to the sight energetically.

In those days piano-wire leaders were unknown, at least to us, and we tied trolling spoons direct to the line. My father would go into a frenzy of orders calculated to get the dragging trolling spoons as far away from the swimming billfish as possible. Because if one did bite, he would thrash to get free, and in his efforts his bill and his teeth would saw the line through in a matter of seconds. You would be out a good trolling spoon. And a good trolling spoon in those days sometimes cost a whole quarter. And quarters were hard come by.

Knowing what had been the cause of our problem had a fine effect on our morale. We knew what to look for and we saw a whole lot of billfish at varying distances from the canoe. We'd point them out to each other.

Looking out to the side for billfish, Sid grew careless and, all of a sudden, again came the explosion and the startled yelp. Our new-found confidence may have lessened the effect of this on Sid, but if so it was scarcely noticeable. He took it nearly as big as he had the first time.

I took over the bow seat, determined I would not be caught off guard. But I grew more and more confident and inattentive. And when the explosion came it was as much of an emotional experience as before, completely unexpected.

That, with minor variations, became the billfish pattern for the rest of the trip up the river. After a billfish explosion we'd paddle gingerly for a short time and be very watchful. Gradually we'd relax. And when we least expected it the next explosion would occur. It was a good thing that Sid and I were young and that our hearts were good. A cardiac case in the bow of our canoe that day wouldn't have survived ten minutes.

At noon we went ashore and ate our lunch. Shortly after lunch we arrived at the basin below the falls in Vergennes. I had been across the bridge above the falls many times, but I had never seen the bridge and the falls from the basin below. It gave me a completely different idea of the lay of the land.

We landed on the left bank where Water Street dips down next to the river. This was where Commodore Thomas Macdonough built the United States war fleet during the War of 1812. When he reached the area, the trees were standing in the forest. And forty-two days later he sailed down the Otter to the lake with a fleet complete. A short while later his fleet met and defeated the British fleet in the Battle of Lake Champlain.

We walked up the hill and along Main Street to Warner's Drug Store where we sat on spindle-legged, ice-cream-parlor stools and ordered sundaes.

And unlike so many things in life, the realization

proved to be every bit as pleasant as the anticipation. We had *big* scoops of ice cream, lots of syrup and chopped nuts with gobs of marshmallow fluff on top. The whole creation contained an astronomical number of calories about which Sid and I knew nothing and cared less. We ate slowly, savoring every delicious spoonful. But all too soon the bottom of the dish appeared.

We started back down the river, full of vigor, refreshed. We had more encounters with exploding billfish, and more interesting conversations, at times, desultory, at times animated.

We passed into Lake Champlain and shortly stopped for another swim. We had various small adventures as we retraced our course of the morning. We began to feel, then, the skin-tightening that comes from too much sun. We had supposed we were, by that time of summer, tanned and immune. But a whole day in the sun, and on the water where reflected rays raise havoc even under a hat, had taught us we weren't as immune as we had hoped.

About six o'clock we landed below our cottage and disembarked, stiff, tired, but inclined to feel that it had been a fine trip and worth while. This feeling grew as time healed tired sore muscles and sunburn, and left nothing to remind us of the less pleasant things that had happened to us.

Gradually it became a *very* wonderful trip: we talked about doing it again the next year.

3

"The Wind She Blow on Lac Champlain"

Air pollution was a real problem even when I was young. But we didn't recognize it as a problem. In those days there were no anti-burning laws, and science hadn't yet invented ways of cutting down on the black smoke belching from factory chimneys.

Pittsburgh in particular was notorious for its black factory smoke. Cartoonists, joke writers, vaudeville (remember it?) comedians used to have a heyday poking fun at poor Pittsburgh. One cartoon showed a V of white birds with one coal-black bird who looked the worse for wear among the white ones, and the caption was, "I flew down by way of Pittsburgh."

In autumn on a still night when everybody had been burning leaves, the smoke was everywhere until you could hardly see. But the leaf smoke on the heavy air of a still, warm autumn evening, we loved.

If there's one smell in the world that more than any other brings back the bittersweet memories of childhood's days, it's the smell of burning leaves. One whiff of it will transport me instantly more than fifty years back to a more leisurely, less crowded, quieter era when people stayed at home a lot more and didn't zip off in every direction at the slightest pretext. It acts like a science-fiction time machine on me. It was a pungent, delightful aroma, and people used to sit on their porches in the evening and smile contentedly when the smell reached them.

19

As for air pollution's effect on us, in my opinion it was negligible. On two or three evenings a year conditions would be right for leaf smoke to hang low; the rest of the evenings you'd get just a tantalizing whiff of it now and then. And you never hear jokes about Pittsburgh now. It has rid itself of coal smoke and acquired smog from car exhausts just like the other cities, so Pittsburgh isn't funny any more.

But the critical factor was that there were very few gasoline engines spewing out exhaust fumes in the air. There were one or two of the newfangled automobiles in each small town, certainly no more than six in a larger town. The cities had more, but only because there was a far greater concentration of people in a city.

Horses still took each meeting with a car very big indeed. My grandmother had a Morgan horse named Pony that was fairly typical. If Pony met a car when she was fresh and just leaving home, she'd try wholeheartedly to climb a telephone pole, or a tree or a fence. If she'd been on the road an hour or two she'd lay her ears back and rear up on her hind legs, then run at breakneck speed once she was past. But if she had been on a long trip and the barn was only a short distance farther on, Pony would pay no attention whatever to a passing car.

What few motorboats there were, were called "naphtha launches." And they all had inboard motors; the outboard motor was a contraption which somebody had just invented and which everybody knew of course would never work, or amount to anything if it did.

Unless there was a forest fire, or you visited Pittsburgh, or passed a rendering plant or a creamery which let its waste flow out and down the hill in back of the plant, air pollution was just no problem.

We owned neither a car nor a motorboat. But my father and the friends who came to visit us in the summer had these two modern conveniences in mind. Each summer we would rent a seven-passenger car one full day

bow for a boat her size. Items crashed onto the floor in the cabin; some of them broke.

The boat rode high on the next wave, slid down into the trough and buried its nose in the next. That time spray came clear over the top deck and onto all of us in the after cockpit.

There was a good deal of yelling and screaming, then. My father cut down on the speed. Uncle Fred jumped for the motor. After that the boat no longer plunged deep into each oncoming wave. But we didn't move forward much, either.

Why had the amount of wind and the size of the waves increased so dramatically when we rounded Split Rock Mountain? Because the ten-mile sweep which a north wind gets in our part of the lake is nothing when compared to the fifty-mile sweep it gets there in the broad lake. When we looked to the north there was nothing visible but horizon and a few islands. That, and huge waves. It would amaze you how large, with so much sweep, waves can become in only a moderate wind.

We continued on at the very slow speed we were now going, and the men held a council of war.

My father said, "I think we ought to turn around."

Since everybody was by then good and scared, nobody gave him even a minor argument. But the next problem was how to go about it.

It had become plain to all the adults in just that few minutes that whereas the boat was very adequate in the smaller areas of the lake, when confronted with any real weather she was unseaworthy and tended to wallow. Also, at that slow speed, she was very sluggish about answering her helm.

My father laid out the problem for us.

"If she gets sideways in the trough of waves like these I'd be afraid she might even tip over. As long as we keep her bow into the wind and don't speed up, we're pretty safe. But we'd have to turn her sideways in turning

23

her around. And once sideways, she might not answer her helm even as well as she's answering it now. There'd be a few minutes, too, until we got up speed in the other direction, when water might come in over the transom."

We kids were all for keeping on; this was still just an exciting adventure as far as we were concerned. But in those days kids did not make the family decisions: it was decided to turn around. We'd get behind the mountain and wait for the wind to die down.

"We'll try to find an area of smaller waves ahead. And when they reach us, everybody will have to be braced for the roll and we'll turn as fast as we can. We'll just hope we're not crossways in the trough when the next big wave hits us."

It was decided that we'd speed up as we started to turn to give the rudder a chance to take hold quicker and more efficiently.

Then came the anxious wait for the lull in the big waves for which we were looking. Even the young fry were becoming conscious of the feeling of danger and tension in the adults. The wait was agonizingly long. We'd look ahead anxiously. But if there were one or two smaller waves, they would be *only* one or two, and would be followed immediately by huge rollers. My father was at the helm and Uncle Fred was in the cabin with the motor.

Finally, though, when we had about given up hope, there appeared ahead quite a series of smaller waves, and my father tensed.

When we hit the first of them he spun the wheel and the motor speeded up. With agonizing slowness the bow turned. For a long time we seemed to be quartering the wind, and then we were finally in the trough and rolling alarmingly.

All this had taken, I suppose, only a matter of seconds. But the smaller waves were fast passing underneath us. And behind them there was a lake full of huge waves which seemed to me to be rushing to get at us while we were still vulnerable.

As we lay in the trough the craft seemed slower than ever about answering her helm. A big wave loomed above us and the boat seemed to flirt its tail in that direction, so we were again quartering the wind, this time with our stern toward it.

The wave broke partly over us, and cold lake water drenched everything in the cockpit. Another wave loomed.

Again the flirt of the tail as we slid down the wave. And we were at last stern to the waves. That wave broke over us but not as badly as the previous one, because the boat had begun to pick up way and to travel with the wind. We almost kept out from under that one.

Then the third wave came along. We were picking up speed and we rose on that wave. It reached for us but did not get us. We climbed to its top and slid down the other side.

There wasn't much time to feel relieved. There was a lot of bailing to be done and we all pitched in and did it. The boat had no automatic bailer and we had to lift some of the floorboards to get at the water which the waves had dumped upon us. There was considerable water sloshing in the bilge. Worst of all, the engine began to skip alarmingly from time to time, probably from wet wiring. And when it did that, there were a lot of hearts that skipped a beat too.

But the motor always caught again, and now that we were moving with the wind there was little danger so long as it kept on going. The skiff we were towing had threatened to come into the cockpit with us during the turn, but Mr. Lake—Uncle Harry—had fended it off successfully, and now it was swinging from side to side behind us, riding high.

We approached the mountain and edged over a little to swing in behind it. And suddenly everything was calm and placid and mill-pondish. It was hard to believe that moving a few hundred feet into the lee of a mountain could bring such a change.

We cruised back along the mountain in calm water past the lighthouse and its cove and dock, until we came to Grog Harbor, a tiny, almost landlocked cove. My father had been there before. Now that we had decided to wait in that area for less wind, he headed directly for it.

If you had written specifications for a perfect spot to wait out a spell of wind, you could not have improved upon Grog Harbor. The entrance was deep, between two huge rocks. You could dive safely off either of those rocks into deep water. Directly opposite the entrance there was a tiny sand beach, and a narrow cleared field which rose gradually toward the top of the mountain. Near the top of the field there had once been a house which had burned, leaving only the fireplace and chimney standing.

On the left side of the harbor there was a dock that had evidently belonged to the place with the chimney. The planking that had formerly covered its top had long since rotted away, but the big timbers which made up the cribbing that held the rock fill in place, were still mostly intact. You could cross the dock's surface by picking your way among the stones of the fill.

We edged the boat in with Uncle Harry standing on the bow to give information about the depth of the water to my father at the wheel. Thus we sidled up to the dock, and fastened our lines there to the ends of the long bolts that held the timbers in place.

After we had tied up we went exploring. In Grog Harbor you would not have known there was even a breeze, to say nothing of waves so big they had threatened to capsize us. We explored the old chimney area and the field, swam and dived from the rocks. We took ashore our bedrolls and spread them, built a fireplace and gathered dry driftwood for the fire. We took ashore the pots and pans and the supplies that the women would need in getting dinner and supper. In those days in rural areas you ate dinner at noon, supper at night.

We tried to do some fishing—without much luck as I remember it. We lay in the sun in our bathing suits. The cooking fire with its attendant smells was a very interesting place, and one which the younger members of the expedition considered it well to keep under close surveillance. We climbed along the rock cliffs, and I remember finding the first bluebells I had ever seen; they seemed to grow out of a minute crack in the solid rock.

After supper, as it grew dark, we built the fire higher (the wood was for the taking) and we reclined around it and talked and even sang for a while.

Nothing unusual about all this, you say: it goes on in campgrounds and at marinas everywhere.

Right. But there was just one difference. All that long afternoon and evening we never saw a single person not of our party. Nor did we ever hear a person. A couple of boats went past the entrance to the harbor, well out, and we neither saw their owners nor were bothered by them. When we wanted drinking water my father took a pail and climbed around the rocks of the entrance, so that the water he got would be from the lake and not the harbor, and dipped up a pailful. We didn't draw chlorinated water from a spigot in the campground, we didn't receive a small bundle of mediocre wood from a caretaker. We didn't disregard any No Trespassing signs, we didn't have to face any irate owner, we didn't have boats, hundreds of boats, anchored in rows near us, no blaring radios or record players, no noise from others, and no others to be disturbed by our subdued singing. In fact *no* others, period. We didn't watch over our things, put anything under lock and key. There just wasn't anybody around; and if there had been, he would have respected our privacy and ownership.

27

We went to bed, some of the women aboard the boat, the rest of us under the stars. As usual, being used to a soft bed, I had trouble getting comfortable the hip I was lying on. For a while there was talking and giggling. Then the next thing I knew it was the middle of the night. The stars above us were still bright, there was the lapping of ripples against the outer rocks, and the realization of where we were suddenly flooded over me. But there was, beside me, the reassuring bulk of my father; I lay there and heard the small night noises, at first with painful alertness, then only jarred from a beginning doze by some extra movement or noise.

The last thing I remember was the sound, far, far away, of a train whistle—a steam whistle, because at that time there were no diesels. Only those who are old enough can understand and appreciate the siren appeal of this night sound. It was mournful and in the small hours it would bring, to the wakeful mind, visions of far places, of world commerce on the move, of adventure. You were safe and drowsy in bed, but here was the reminder that others were up, traveling, carrying on the world's work that still must be done while the rest of the world sleeps. You thought, perhaps, about the other wakeful souls who heard that long wailing sound, some of them perhaps aboard the train itself. You were delighted to be where you were, comfortable and safe, yet you envied them a tiny bit too.

Perhaps the envy was more then than it is now. We traveled very little in comparison with present times, and it was the beckoning call to far places. Perhaps we wanted, each in his subconscious mind, to travel more. All I know is that a train whistle in the night, a steam whistle, was a very haunting thing; to those who haven't experienced the feeling this must be hard to understand. I lay there that night and thought about it and the next thing I knew it was broad daylight.

There was, that morning, the businesslike bustle of breakfast-getting, packing, dismantling the camp. The north wind still held about as strong as the day before, and rather than stay another day in Grog Harbor, it was decided we would go back home. This was a bitter blow to the younger members of the party, bitterly resisted by them. But the decision held.

We embarked toward the middle of the morning, turned the boat around with the ropes, and tried to start the engine. It did not start with the first "twist of its tail" as it usually had, and Uncle Fred did things to it with tools, and looked very harassed. The rest of us waited.

After what seemed like a very long time to us, the thing finally caught. It skipped often, but since it was felt that this would clear up as the wiring dried, we started out. We had progressed only a few hundred yards along the face of the mountain when the engine stopped again and refused to restart.

This was serious now. If it did not start soon we would gradually drift out where the wind would pick us up, and then we would be in several hundred feet of water with no control over where we were drifting. We had no anchor rope *that* long.

My father took one of the skiff's oars, and, using it as a scull, inched us slowly toward the sheer cliff while Uncle Fred worked on the engine. We came closer and closer to the rock until finally we picked out a flat narrow ledge at the water's edge where Uncle Harry and my father could get out and hold the boat instead of using the oar to keep it from drifting. There was, as I have said, maybe two hundred feet of water in front of the cliff of which the shelf was a part.

Still the engine refused to start.

We had been there awhile when suddenly someone pointed out toward open water. Just coming into sight past a jutting point of ledge, was the steamer *Vermont*, the huge side-wheeler that made the run daily from Plattsburgh to Montcalm Landing. She was close in there because the water was so deep.

My father actually turned pale. He alone of all of us

29

realized the danger we were in from the wake of the big steamer. Her very heavy waves could bash us against that ledge, crush us like an eggshell. We would be, very simply, at the mercy of those huge waves.

There was no time to re-embark and try to get far enough away from the rocks with an oar so that we would be safe: the oar had only inched us along on the way in.

My father had to make an instantaneous decision and he decided to stay with the ledge. Uncle Fred was called out from working on the engine. He had been a football player and was very large and strong. He too climbed out onto the ledge. We got pillows, long seat cushions, anything to soften the boat's impact against the ledge. Those of us who weren't on the ledge stood ready to jam things into place where and when padding was needed.

I have thought of it often since, and I have come to realize (which I didn't at the time) how frightened my father was. He was responsible for the safety of all of us and of the boat, and in a few moments we might all be floundering in that very deep water, our boat splintered and sinking. If it sank there was the real danger that the suction of its going might carry many of us under with it, even those of us who could swim well.

We got ourselves braced and waited, grim, frightened.

The waves hit, what little they did hit. And nothing happened. There had to be some holding and some padding. Down the shore a short distance to the west of us those waves thundered devastatingly against the cliff, and spray shot high in air.

But where we were, the suction of the steamer's passing and the return of the water afterward was about the worst thing we had to contend with.

The jutting point of ledge which had kept us from seeing the *Vermont* until she was almost on us, stuck out just far enough to bear the brunt of those waves instead of us. In its lee we got almost nothing.

My father almost collapsed on the ledge when the danger was over. He was a deeply religious man. I know now that he must have prayed; and that he felt our deliverance had been an answer to his prayer.

After many moments of high relief the men went back to the business of getting the motor started.

It started after a long while. We finally left the ledge and started on our way. As we turned Scotch Bonnet and headed south we got farther and farther away from the lee of Split Rock Mountain. The waves grew bigger and bigger. They were never the size of the ones we had encountered in the broad lake, but they were much larger than the ones we had faced the day before when we came north through that area.

However, the motor was running fairly well, and the waves were quartering behind us. All was going well.

And then again the motor stopped.

That time we never did get it started again. The boat promptly turned sideways in the trough of the waves, and rolled and wallowed there alarmingly. This time we were a long distance from land.

Instantly my father grabbed the painter of the skiff, pulled it close, and jumped in. The skiff was double-ended, and by changing and rowing from the second middle seat, you could use the bow for the stern.

He threw me the painter that was already fastened to the bow of the skiff, and then sat so that the bow would be the stern. I sat on the forward deck of the big boat and braced myself. And he started to row.

He pulled the bow of the big boat around so that it faced away from the wind, and at once the wallowing stopped. I tried to fasten the painter to a cleat, but when the slack was suddenly taken out of it after it was hitched solidly, it cracked like a whip and there was very real danger that it might snap in two after a few repetitions of such treatment. It was decided that I should sit there braced, and hold the painter and let out and take in slack to ease that snapping of the rope.

Things went better after that. One minute my father would be higher than I was, the next I'd be looking down at him in that shell of a rowboat.

But things went very well. My father, as I've said, was completely confident of his ability to handle anything he could row. He was rowing now, bringing into play all the tricks he had learned over so many years. He was not trying to tow the big boat as much as he was trying to keep it headed in the direction of the wind so that it would ride the waves well. With what he did manage to do in the way of towing, plus the force of the wind, we made progress.

Only one thing was against us: the wind was blowing from the northeast, not straight from the north. If we went completely with the wind, it would bring us ashore in the Mullen Brook area of the New York shore, and not over on the Vermont side.

At first my father tried to quarter in the direction of our cottage, but matters did not go as well when he did. And all the time the wind took us in its direction instead of in ours. The angle toward camp widened. Finally my father gave up and just kept the boat headed in the direction *it* wanted to go.

Time passed. Uncle Harry and Uncle Fred offered to spell my father at the oars, but he felt there would have been grave danger in trying to make the change with those waves. And I knew that he felt the others had not had the experience behind the oars in that skiff that he had had. The others spelled me at holding the painter.

We got farther and farther south in the lake and closer and closer to the New York shore.

Finally my father called to us, "I think I can make the bay behind Presbrey's Point." And he did just that.

People who had been watching us through the

glasses came down to the shore from the Presbrey cottage. When our predicament had been explained to Mr. Presbrey he offered to take his own launch and tow us over to Vermont. We took him up on his offer and the women rode in the comfort of his launch. Behind the launch was our big boat, and behind it was my father's skiff with him in it. He hadn't intended to be in it, but, riding light, it wandered so much on the end of its painter that it was decided someone should be in it for weight and to steer.

We took the boat back to its usual mooring on the far side of Potash Bay which was shielded from a north wind (our cottage wasn't) and we got everybody and all our things ashore with the skiff.

For years afterward we kept a friendly relationship with the Presbreys on the New York side. Mr. Presbrey would, incidentally, accept no money for his kindness to us. This was not considered out of the ordinary then.

So the trip was a failure, almost a fiasco. But for years I have remembered it as one of the high adventures of my whole life. And judging by the conversations I have had with the others, I'm sure they feel the same way.

Using the motor as little as we did, we polluted the air very little. Our fire at night, if anyone smelled its wood smoke—which I doubt—probably gave the same feeling of well-being that I always get from smelling burning leaves in the fall.

Certainly nobody else's pollution harmed us, except the wave pollution of the lake's surface by wind and by the steamer *Vermont*. No, pollution didn't trouble us much on Lake Champlain in the early 1900's.

4

Total War with an Outboard Motor

Outboard motors furnish the motive power for the majority of the small speedboats which today zip here and there like a bunch of disturbed water bugs on any body of water larger than a postage stamp. They aren't necessarily going anywhere; they're just going. And at a good healthy percentage of the speed of sound, too.

Well, we *did* have an outboard motor. Not at the time we took the abortive trip aboard the cruiser, but a few years afterward. We had what was, as far as I can find out, the first outboard motor ever owned in Addison County, maybe the first ever owned in Vermont. Oh, there was nothing backward about us; no sir, we were right up to date with the rest of them.

Uncle Fred was the one who saw the advertisement in a magazine.

He said to my father, "Prent, look at this. A man has invented a motor for a boat and it hitches on the *outside.* Drives the thing along faster than you can row. And when you don't want to use it you can take it off, and then put it back on when you *do* want to use it. Do you suppose the thing would actually work?"

My father was inclined to think it wouldn't. As I've said, he had great faith in his ability with oars and a paddle.

But Uncle Fred persisted. "There wouldn't be any danger in it. It wouldn't be like that big cruiser." He

34

paused for a moment and you could tell they were both thinking about *that* scare. "If it stopped, all you'd have to do would be to put the oars in the oarlocks and row. There's no reason you couldn't row while the thing—I believe he calls it an 'outboard motor'—was right in place."

It took days and weeks to convince my father. He was skeptical but intrigued. He kept bringing up objections and Uncle Fred kept shooting them full of holes. In order to do this Uncle Fred had to send away for literature on the motor. He had, in other words, to convince himself so that he could convince my father.

"Now, Prent, you say that it would scare all the fish, but look at this testimonial. Mr. B. of Wisconsin says: 'I was afraid that using the motor would scare the fish. But I have caught more fish since using it than I ever caught before.' And Mr. W. of Michigan says: 'Before buying your motor I used to be so tired from rowing to and from my girl's house in the evenings that I was on the verge of losing my job. But after I got the motor, going to visit her was so easy that now I am happily married and just got a big raise.' "

"Humph," my father said; "I get plenty of fish now, I'm already happily married, and it would take more than an outboard motor to get a raise out of Clark University."

But his opposition was eroded gradually after he had read letters from Mr. S. of Washington, and a particularly glowing tribute from Mr. A. of South Carolina that told of a five-day trip he took during which the motor performed almost unbelievable feats and never faltered even once.

"Sounds as if gathering firewood and doing the cooking was the only thing his motor hadn't been able to handle," my father said. "But maybe it was never given a chance. Mr. A. may have *enjoyed* cooking."

However, even though my father made fun of these

letters, they wore away his opposition, each by a little bit. And Uncle Fred kept after him. Finally they sent in the order.

In due course the motor arrived at the railroad station in Vergennes, in a wooden crate. They made the necessary arrangements to have it brought down, and that wasn't easy in those days. It required among other things several phone-use trips to the nearest farmhouse, and much shouting into the mouthpiece and much waving and gesticulating with the arm and hand not holding the receiver.

But finally the motor was delivered. Uncle Fred and my father opened the crate and admired their purchase. My father maintained a skeptical attitude, but it was plain to see that even he was impressed.

"Isn't she a beauty?" Uncle Fred said reverently.

And my father said, "Humph! Beauty is as beauty does."

"You'll see, Prent. We'll just take it down to the beach, put it on the boat, and go for a little spin."

There turned out, however, to be problems. And the first problem that reared its ugly head had to do with the clamps. The motor clamps had been designed to fit a boat with a square stern. My father's skiff was V-ended. They puzzled over this for a while, but even two men who knew as little about mechanical matters as they did, could see what they were up against.

"We'll have to do something about those clamps before it will fit on the boat," Uncle Fred admitted grudgingly. "It's a cinch it isn't going to fit the way it is."

Many times since, I've seen outboard motors that have been attached to V-ended boats. Usually there is a metal or wooden frame that sticks out at the stern at right angles to the forward line of the boat. The motor is clamped to this and rides a little to the right of center with a right-handed operator. Why Uncle Fred and my father did not think of making such a frame I do not know, but they didn't. Instead they took the problem to a blacksmith-machinist, and he came up with a set of clamps and clamp-seats that allowed the motor to be mounted directly on the V stern. This necessitated a delay of almost a week and several trips with Pony hitched to the farm wagon to carry the motor to the blacksmith shop and get it back again when the job was done.

This delay gave Uncle Fred and my father a chance to do something about dry-cells. There were wires with the motor, and in the directions there were explicit instructions for fastening them to the dry-cells. Then there was a note that said DRY-CELLS NOT FURNISHED. My father sputtered about this. Perhaps it would have made him feel better if he had known that in the years to come, when I bought toys for my daughter and later still for my grandchildren, I invariably opened the package to find a note saying BATTERIES NOT FURNISHED. This would lead me to wonder if, in Roman times, when a man bought a toy catapult for his son, there was not a papyrus note to the effect that "batteryae non furnishum est."

With the motor in position there was the problem of where to put the package of dry-cells once they had been purchased. The V-stern seat was covered by a fitted board which acted as a brace for the sides, a cover for the back end of the seat, and a backrest. The logical place for the batteries was on the seat, but my father took a dim view of removing this fitted board.

"What are you going to lean against if you do?" he asked.

It was eventually decided to bore a hole in the board for the wires to go through. This would fix it so that the dry-cells could be placed on the seat under cover in back of the operator as he steered the boat.

The motor did not look like any outboard motor you see today. And principally this was because there was no flywheel. In place of a flywheel, around which in later models you wound a starter rope, the shaft stuck up with two nubs poking out near the top. Over this you were supposed to fit a crank which *was* furnished.

In fact two cranks were furnished.

My father said, "Why *two?* You couldn't ever lose anything as big as *that.*"

In due course we found out why two cranks. But in the meantime there were directions to be pored over, oil to be purchased, gasoline to be bought (and of course a can to carry it in). Finally the big day arrived when we would try out our new acquisition.

Under the watchful eye of Uncle Fred—who stood there holding the directions and other papers in one hand, pointing here and there with the other, wearing a worried look—we got everything in place and pushed off. I rowed out far enough so we would have plenty of water to maneuver in when the boat leaped ahead. Uncle Fred was in the stern seat so that he could handle the motor, my father was in the sternmost of the middle seats so he could help if needed, and I sat in the rowing seat. This of course did not trouble me at all because there would be no rowing.

"Everybody ready?" Uncle Fred asked. We agreed that we were. He grasped the crank-handle and spun the motor.

The motor backfired, kicked; the crank was ripped from his hand, shot through the air and disappeared into the water.

Uncle Fred yelled, "Ouch!" feelingly, along with some other words. And he held his thumb in his other hand reproachfully. One of his least flowery remarks was, "Boy, this thing has got a kick like a mule."

Since we now had no crank, I rowed ashore to get the spare.

"But," my father said, "won't it happen again?"

"No," Uncle Fred explained, "I had the spark advanced too far. That will sometimes cause a motor to kick. I'll retard the spark a little. And I'll be on the lookout. I'll hold the crank-handle with my thumb on the same side my fingers are on. They say that when you crank a car you should always keep your thumb on the same side of the crank-handle your fingers are on, else you're likely to get it broken."

In the days before self-starters, when you cranked a car with a crank that disengaged and hung right there under your radiator, this bit of operational procedure was known to everyone; if you owned a car and didn't know it, you soon found it out, afterward carrying your arm in a sling. It's also been many years since motors had a lever with which you advanced or retarded the spark.

After we had procured the second crank—we now had the question answered about why they furnished two—I rowed the few strokes that would take us back where we had been.

Uncle Fred said, "Ready?" And he twisted the crank.

The motor backfired, kicked; the crank shot sideways and disappeared into the water. Uncle Fred spoke various words, phrases, even clauses. The only difference between this time and the first time was that he didn't say "Ouch." He had kept his thumb out of harm's way.

We went ashore again. We pulled the boat up on shore. We got into bathing suits and came back down to the beach to dive for the cranks. The water was reasonably shallow and we found them both without much trouble.

We tried again the next day. That time Uncle Fred was ready. He twisted the crank, the motor kicked, Uncle Fred hung on to the crank. The next time the motor neither backfired nor kicked; it also didn't start. It sulked and did nothing. Obviously it felt that Uncle Fred had stopped playing the game fair.

Uncle Fred cranked and cranked. Nothing. My father cranked and cranked. Nothing. Uncle Fred again.

Nothing. My father again. The motor kicked, the crank disappeared into the water.

It was decided that we needed expert help and advice. Fred Smith, a boyhood friend of my father's, was the man we decided to consult. He lived about two miles away and owned one of the few cars in the neighborhood. After we had recovered the crank by diving again, we phoned him and my father placed our problem before him.

Mr. Smith arrived carrying some tools and was taken directly to the beach. He seemed extremely interested in the motor, looked it over minutely, saying under his breath several times, "What won't they think of next?"

He checked various items, nodded, shook the wires, nodded some more.

Finally he turned to my father and said, "There isn't any reason why it shouldn't start, Prent. Let's give it a whirl."

It was decided that four would overload the boat and I was sent out to row Mr. Smith a couple of dozen feet from shore and hold the boat in place while he cranked. Uncle Fred, who worried, called out to us, "Watch out for that crank!" He unconsciously held his right thumb with his left hand.

A boy has sharp eyes and notices a lot more than anybody gives him credit for even seeing. I noticed that Mr. Smith set the gas and spark levers exactly where Uncle Fred and my father had set them. I also noticed that he kept his thumb on the same side of the crank-handle that his fingers were on.

"Be ready to ship those oars when she starts," he said. I didn't say anything but I had some definite ideas about its starting.

Mr. Smith twisted the crank; the motor started. I had to scramble plenty to get the oar blades out of water, so sure had I been that it wouldn't start.

We whizzed back and forth across in front of the landing. "Whizzed" is a relative term. The speed at which we traveled would certainly not be called whizzing today. But we traveled faster than I had ever before traveled in a rowboat and as far as I was concerned it was whizzing. I let out a "Yippee" or two.

After a short while Mr. Smith turned the boat toward shore, shut off the motor and coasted in.

"A nice-running little motor, Prent," he said.

"What did you do to it?" my father asked.

"Nothing. I set everything just the way the directions say." I could have borne witness that this was true.

Uncle Fred went out next with Mr. Smith. Uncle Fred cranked, the motor started with the first turn. They rode around a few minutes, then came back to shore. My father went out with Mr. Smith, started the motor the first time, rode around a bit and came back to shore.

"I guess that licks it," my father said. "I'm sorry we didn't try once more before we called you, Fred. Thanks ever so much for coming." Mr. Smith took his departure.

"Now," my father said, "we'll take the ladies out for a spin."

My father loaded the ladies, put me in the rowing seat to get the boat out away from shore, then turned the crank. The motor started instantly, and we were off.

Everybody enjoyed the incredible speed—we were moving almost one-and-a-half times as fast as my father could row—and we were all excited about this new mode of transportation.

Opposite Potash Point, some two miles from the cottage, the motor skipped, then sputtered on for a few seconds, then stopped.

"Oops," my father said; "I'll restart it."

He cranked. Nothing happened. He cranked again. And again. And again. Still nothing. He may have cranked fifty times when the motor suddenly kicked, backfired. And the crank shot off to one side and disappeared in twenty or thirty feet of water about half a mile from shore.

My father and I very gingerly and carefully changed places and he rowed home. As for that crank, it was a goner. The water was too deep to dive for it even if we had had any way of marking for sure where it disappeared. We never saw *that* crank again.

From then on we were at the tender mercies of the world's most temperamental motor. If we didn't care whether the motor started or not, it would start. If it had us some place where stopping would be an embarrassment or worse, it would stop. If it stopped, and failing to start again would be at all inconvenient, it most assuredly would fail to start.

Of course the first problem that confronted us, being down to one crank, was how to avoid getting down to no cranks at all. After all, it was obviously impossible always to start the motor in water shallow enough for us to dive and get the crank again.

This meant another trip to the blacksmith. He agreed to make a hole in the handle of the old crank so we could attach a rope to it. At the same time he took a pattern of the old crank and promised to make one to replace the one we had lost.

With a cord tied through the new hole in the crank-handle and the other end of the cord fastened securely to the gunwale of the skiff, we won an important battle in the war with the motor. I'll never forget the look of supreme, smug triumph on Uncle Fred's face the first time the crank was wrenched from his hand after that. As he retrieved it by pulling in the rope hand-over-hand like someone bringing in a minnow bucket, he addressed the motor personally and out loud. "There, I fooled you didn't I, damn you," he gloated. "You thought the defense couldn't catch up with the offense, didn't you?" As I've said, Uncle Fred was football-minded.

It was an eventful and unusual summer. There is a

maxim which says that if you build a better mousetrap the world will beat a path to your door. My father said that he had developed a new maxim: if you own a worse motor, Fred Smith will beat a path to your door.

Fred Smith appeared often at the cottage that summer, always by request. Always it would be after many hours (or even days) of fruitless cranking. Mr. Smith would do things like taking out the spark plug and cleaning it, or changing the gap, and immediately the motor would start as if it were a small puppy bent on pleasing its master.

Mr. Smith told us, among other things, that in his opinion the lack of a flywheel was what caused the motor to stop so often. It would skip and there'd be no momentum to carry it along till it fired again. This has always seemed reasonable to me; the motors today that never falter, have flywheels.

We tried to use the motor in trolling, but it made the boat skitter off across the water like a scared duck.

"It seems to go," my father said disgustedly, "about twice as fast throttled down as it does wide open." My father had taken to using motor language with the best of them.

We solved that problem by tying a rope to the bail of an empty bucket and dragging it behind the boat. This slowed things down to trolling speed, believe me. But the progress of the pail through the water must have intrigued the fish, or scared them, or something, because my father began to feel he was fishing for nothing, and any such feeling was poison to him. After that he rowed for trolling. This was a battle won by the motor.

There was one time when we'd have sworn the motor would refuse to run, and perversely it ran beautifully.

In a storm we offered to tow a big flat-bottomed, awkward boat against a very heavy wind when the city man who was trying to row it had been forced ashore because he was losing footage as he rowed.

We tossed him a rope and half expected our motor to stop forthwith. But it kept right on chugging.

Between the force of the wind and the weight of the big hulk behind us, we were right away aware of a very peculiar thing. The water rushed past us all right, its waves driven by the strong winds, but when we sighted against the shoreline, we weren't moving anywhere.

"Prent," Uncle Fred said, "we're just barely holding our own."

"Nonsense," my father said. "Why, the motor's running like a dream." He rapped on the wooden gunwale—rapped on wood—immediately to be on the safe side. "We'll get straightened around right off, then you'll see."

We may have got straightened around, but we didn't go anywhere. The same reddish rock continued to be right opposite us on shore.

"You're right, Fred," my father said. "You know what I'm going to do? I'm going to row."

He got the oars into the oarlocks. And with the motor holding us even against the wind and storm and the weight of the hulk, my father's efforts at the oars were rewarded as if he were rowing in a flat calm with *nothing* in tow. We were able to make good time in delivering the other boat to its destination and getting ourselves back to the cottage. But we must have presented a rather startling appearance to anyone watching—Uncle Fred running the motor full speed and my father rowing hard besides. It must have been calculated to shake one's faith in modern inventions.

Gradually, in dealing with the motor, my father and Uncle Fred developed a low cunning. This was done as the result of trial and error. We didn't win all the battles, but we found out how to win some of them. For instance, there was a whole list of things that the two of them could remember having done at various times just before the motor started. Once they had wrapped a life preserver around it; once they had turned the throttle on and off three times just before they cranked it; once they had moved the batteries from one side of the seat to the other and back again; once my father had put a special old hat on just before they attained success. All these things were remembered and each added to the list. When the time came to crank they'd go through the whole list; they didn't dare leave any item out because that might be the one thing that was helping them.

And, by golly, it worked more times than not. Fred Smith snorted at the list, but until someone came up with a plan that worked better, my father and Uncle Fred continued to wrap the life preserver into place and do the other things. And start the motor.

And my father, after many frustrating attempts to take people out for a ride only to have the motor refuse to start, had a sure-fire answer to *that* problem.

He'd leave the party sitting on the porch of the cottage and go down to the beach. He'd tie the skiff's rope around his waist and then wade out with the boat to reasonably deep water. Standing there he'd try to crank the motor.

If it failed to start, he never said anything to his guests about a ride. No harm was done; no face was lost.

But if the motor started, he'd run the boat empty in a circle around him at the end of the rope until he was pretty sure it would keep running. Then he'd call to my mother and she'd ask the guests if they'd like to go for an outboard-motor ride.

They'd come down to the beach. My father would take the boat and nose it into the beach with the motor still running; he'd load the party.

Then, still in the water up to his middle, he'd manage to move the boat out, turn it, climb into the stern, advance the throttle and they'd be off. Sometimes he'd be rowing when they returned, but at least this method assured him of a good start.

So, as I say, we won some of the battles, and lost some

of them. Neither my father nor the motor won the war.

The summer ended with the Hoyts down to one crank (the rope had broken one time)—and with the contest a stalemate. We went back to Worcester for the winter, leaving the motor locked in the woodshed.

When we returned the next summer, the woodshed had been broken into and the motor (and only the motor) had been taken.

My father said, "Well, the motor's gone." And he must have been a very stoical man. Because, in spite of this rather severe financial loss, he smiled almost all day.

Shortly after that he wrote Uncle Fred and told him that a thief now had possession of our motor. In a couple of days a telegram reached us from Uncle Fred. It was short and concise:

"Serves him right."

5

Fishing for Food and Fun

Every morning except Sundays we went fishing.

By that I don't mean every morning that we didn't have something more important to do. Or that somebody didn't feel well, or that it didn't rain, or that the north wind didn't blow. We went *every* morning. About the only exceptions were for our annual automobile trip into the Adirondacks, and the one time we took the cruiser up the lake.

How did it happen that I let my father regiment my life and dictate to me that way? Why didn't I protest? Why didn't I refuse to go?

Well, there were several reasons, but the main one was that my father might have said, "Fine. Stay home." And I didn't *want* to stay home. I wanted to go fishing.

I've mentioned that our trolling every morning was on our trip across the bay to get the milk. My father, especially if we had female guests, would sometimes treat this as a terrible chore, for the record: "I wish I could stay here and help entertain Mrs. Jones, but I've got to make that darned trip over after the milk."

My mother was never taken in by this—they understood each other—or by my claim that I had to go too because the skiff didn't trim well or row easily if there was no weight in the stern.

My father liked an eight o'clock start for the trip. And at about ten minutes of eight he would begin to fret, would look at his watch. He'd go down to the beach, load the skiff, test his lines. He'd find the milk pail and its cover, he'd get the fish bag. He wouldn't *say* anything to anybody; just be around looking at his watch.

Sure enough, people would start to hurry, would practically race just at the end. And at eight o'clock we'd be pushing off.

How could we ever expect to catch anything with the primitive equipment available to us then? Well, even before monofilament line, spinning reels, fiberglass rods, electronic fish-finders, sophisticated lures were any of them discovered, we did pretty well.

What sort of rods did we use? We didn't use rods. We used poles. Great long bamboo poles twenty-five feet from tip to butt. We bought them at Dalrymple's Store in Vergennes. We always bought the longest ones we could buy. They cost us twenty-five cents each.

Nor did we use reels. We tied a heavy green line direct to the poles so that there would be about three feet more line dangling than there would be length to the pole. We tied the line about six feet back from the tip and then wound it around that upper six feet of pole and fastened it in such a way that it would dangle from the tip. In that way, if a foot or two of the tip broke, we would still have our fish and line and lure securely attached to a heavy part of the pole.

These poles we stuck out almost at right angles to the skiff, one on each side. At the business end of the line we tied a swivel and to the swivel we attached a trolling spoon.

An amazing, primitive outfit? Don't laugh till I've had a chance to explain how it worked and why.

When we started out we set those poles down in place, out across the gunwale. But we held on to the spoons. When the boat had reached deep enough water, and was moving fast enough so the spoons wouldn't sink, we placed them in the water and they'd swing around behind the poles, and we'd be trolling. No letting out a lot of line from a reel, no catching on the bottom. Simple and easy.

If you caught a weed you simply raised the pole straight up in the air, got hold of the end of the line, and then set the pole down in place and held it with your knees. Then, with both hands free, you took off the weed. You set the spoon back in the water, and again you were trolling. With a reel you'd have had to wind all that line in, take off the weed, and then let the line out again. And you'd probably have caught another weed while you were doing it.

Why couldn't we have stayed out deeper where there weren't any weeds? We could have, all right. The problem was that there weren't any northern pike where there weren't any weeds.

At that time Lake Champlain grew beds of weeds fairly close to shore in eight to ten feet of water. Minnows hid in the weeds, larger fish came there for the minnows.

And big northern pike hid deep in the weeds to grab *them.* These weed beds are mostly gone now, the victims of the speedboat. The blossoms of these weeds used to bend over and float on the surface by mid-July, then pollen from them would float to other weed beds. But when outboard speedboats came along, their propellers ripped up the weed blossoms and cut back the stalk. Weeds with surface blossoms produced fewer and fewer seed pods that came to maturity. Gradually the older weeds died off. In the last twenty years it has become increasingly difficult to find a weed bed of the old type.

In my early years at the cottage, though, they flourished. And the idea in northern pike-fishing was to put a trolling spoon—two if possible—across each of those weed beds as we came to it, without getting the spoon weed-fouled so that it would no longer wobble or spin or whatever it was supposed to do to look alluring to a big fish.

If you used a reel, two things were against you. With a casting rod of ordinary length and a short line the big pike would, a moment before, have seen the shadow of the boat pass over, would be skeptical and would not grab the lure when it followed. And if you put out enough line so the pike would no longer associate the lure with the boat's shadow, you'd have your lure running so deep it would catch the first weed it came to in a weed bed. By the time you'd reeled *that* in and let the line out again you'd be past the weed bed in barren territory. You'd be fishing barren territory almost exclusively.

With our bamboo pole outriggers, on the other hand, the shadow of the boat would pass more than twenty feet away from any pike lying below where the lure was going to appear. Your lure would run close to the surface, being on a short line, and would for that reason avoid most of the mass of weeds below.

But if you did hook a weed you could lift your pole,

50

take the weed off, release the lure and be fishing again in the same weed bed, all in a matter of seconds. Our system boiled down to more seconds of operation for each lure in each weed bed.

How did I know that it worked this way? My father experimented endlessly one year with a line in back of the boat while the outriggers were in place out at each side. Each of the outriggers outcaught the line in back of the boat by more than three to one.

We'd troll along and maybe over in the corner of the bay in a big weed bed we'd get a strike on one of the outriggers. Playing and landing a fish without a reel on one of those bamboo outriggers was, as I look back on it, absolutely unbelievable. Today's sportsman would shudder, turn the eyes away, curl the lip. Our city visitors did exactly that. But if they refused to fish the way my father wanted it done, they didn't go out with *him*. He'd furnish them a boat, but he'd never row them.

The first thing you learned was not to do anything except hold that pole-butt solid against an oarlock on the gunwale. Above all you weren't to try to set the hook when you had a strike. A big pike would hit that moving lure like a load of bricks. Pike swallow a victim headfirst, so if the hook was going to get set, the pike would strictly set it himself on that strike. All you'd do if you tried to help set it would be to rip it out of his mouth.

You just braced and hung on to the pole-butt. It was hard just to sit there, but that's what you had to do. That long, limber bamboo pole would bend with every lunge the fish made, sometimes bend almost double. My father would swing the stern of the boat to foil the fish when he lunged either left or right and threatened to get a solid pull off the end of the pole.

The person who was running the other outrigger would lift his pole straight up in the air to keep the hook from catching bottom now that we were stopped. If my father was the one handling the other outrigger and

51

rowing too, he'd just throw the pole overboard. We'd come back for it when the excitement was over, since having no reel, it would float buoyantly. The main thing was to keep it out of the way.

Gradually the fish would tire. My father would try, if the fish would let him, to move out into deep water where there would be no weeds that the line and the fish would slice into and, in doing so, add to the strain on the equipment.

My father was in no hurry. But when the fish definitely began to give up, he'd give the word, and if I was the one who had the fish on, I'd work the pole forward on the gunwale a little. Then I'd slide it across the gunwale and into the water on the opposite side until I could get hold of the line.

With the line between my thumb and first finger I'd bring the fish in toward the boat. When he pulled I'd grudgingly let the line go through my fingers. When he stopped pulling I'd bring him in some more. I'd continue to play him this way. The object was to get him up next to the boat, tired out. We didn't own a landing net. The idea was to squeeze his neck and lift him over the side with one hand.

You had to be careful and know what you were doing. But you weren't working anywhere near those teeth of his, which are something. A pike's teeth are set on one-way hinges. They lie down when anything goes into his mouth, but will not lie down when anything tries to come out again. And they're *sharp*.

Finally I'd have him next to the boat and I'd reach down to squeeze my hand around his neck, my fingers pressing in against his gill covers. This was the most delicate maneuver of all: you just placed your hand a quarter of an inch from the place you intended to squeeze, then suddenly you squeezed. But many of our guests would hold their hands a foot away and make a lunge. The fish would see the lunge coming and react. And when he did that, the guest's other hand on the line would freeze tight closed. Result, a lost fish. Any time your fish got a good solid pull for any reason, the hook was likely to rip out.

I told you the landing process was unbelievable. But it worked. And the outriggers got fish to bite; a whole lot of fish. But just imagine any of your friends today throwing a rod overboard. Unthinkable, even.

When we had the fish, my father would put him in a burlap bag we had brought along, and would wet the bag so that the scales would not dry out and make dressing him difficult. I would retrieve my outrigger and set it back in its fishing position. If my father had tossed the other outrigger overboard we'd go back and retrieve it. And in a few minutes we'd be trolling again.

On these daily fishing excursions we'd have any- where from one to five people in the skiff, depending on whether or not we had company. If it was just one—if my father was making the trip alone, which seldom hap- pened if I could help it—he'd set the two outrigger butts in loops of rope tied to each gunwale. Each pole would then extend out across the opposite gunwale in fishing position, held firm against a spare oarlock. The two butts crossed each other between the gunwales. This left both my father's hands free for rowing, yet the pole-butts in their slings were within his easy reach.

Needless to say, when he was fishing alone that way, he was busier than that one-armed paperhanger with the hives that you're always hearing about. If he got a weed he had to stop rowing, raise the pole, get hold of the lure, reset the pole, free the lure of the weed, grab the oars and start rowing again all before the other lure had sunk low enough to catch bottom. If he caught a fish he had to flip away the other pole and move with his hooked fish to the stern so the wind would turn the boat, taking the place of an oarsman to a small degree, while he played the fish and brought him in. As I say, luckily he didn't have to do this often.

When he and I fished together, which was how I enjoyed it most, I took care of one outrigger and my father set the other one. He was busy then, but nothing like when he was fishing alone.

If my mother fished with us, she and I each handled a bamboo pole, and my father handled the oars and the boat. And everybody had an easy time. If we had a guest he would handle one outrigger, and if there were two guests they'd handle both outriggers, my mother would handle the hand-line directly behind the boat, and I'd be relegated to the bow seat with nothing to do except ride and wish the guests would go home.

We weren't the only ones who used the long bamboo poles. The local farmers, fishing on Sundays or when it rained and they couldn't hay, all used them.

Rowing a boat for this kind of trolling was an art. You had to know exactly how fast to go to keep the action of your spoons as near perfect as possible. You had to memorize each weed bed so that when you had passed over one you could change course and bring your spoons over the next one. Sometimes the turn would have to be almost right-angled. Many times I've seen my father row around an area when the water was clear, studying and memorizing the contour of some weed bed so he could fish it better when the water wasn't clear. He didn't get much chance to do more than row when we were having a lot of company, and he got his satisfaction from maneuvering the boat so expertly that it would catch more pike than any other boat that was out that day.

We didn't fish long hours. We'd stop for the milk on the way home, and arrive back at the cottage in plenty of time to care for our fish and to swim before the noon meal.

This might or might not be the end of fishing for the day, depending on what other plans we had. If we fished again it would be about four o'clock in the afternoon and might take the form of more trolling, or might take the form of still-fishing.

Still-fishing got its name because the boat remained still in one place. We anchored over some likely spot and fished with hand-lines, using worms for bait.

This type of fishing, as I mentioned, brought us perch, sheepshead, bass. We also caught bullpout, mullet, eel, mooneyes, walleyes and a few other varieties. However, perch were caught in the greatest numbers, with sheepshead 'way behind in second place.

Perch, a comparatively small fish, made a very pleasant menu change. When we had company we'd have to catch a lot of perch to make a whole meal. The company was likely to be a bit inept at helping with the catching, too. As a rule-of-thumb my father could outcatch me two to one, and I could outcatch any guest we had by at least that much. This came of experience and practice: experience in presenting your bait, in moving your line, in "trying" it; experience in keeping the fish moving up without slack in the line after you had hooked him.

Dressing enough perch for eight or ten people was no light task. Here, some of the guests were a real help. Sid Gage became adept at the job, and Uncle Harry and Uncle Fred visited us often enough so that they, too, improved their fish-dressing skills a great deal.

There is one extra process in dressing perch which doesn't take a lot longer, but makes a 50 percent improvement in the eating. This process rips off the rib bones and the tiny bones that stick straight out from the top of the ribs. You lose very little edible flesh by doing this. And you end up with only the backbone to contend with when you have finished. If you have eaten many perch you know what a blessing that would be: two slabs of boneless meat, one on each side of the backbone.

The process is not difficult. Skin and dress the perch just as you always do. But then hold the dressed fish in your left hand, ribs up, head end toward you. With your knife in your right hand, cut in toward the backbone at the vent area. Then pull the blade of the knife forward, first on one side, then on the other, at an angle that will sever the rib bones and take out the small bones too. This whole mass of tiny bones will come away in one piece with a little practice. That glob of flesh and bones which you cut off is considered to be a great delicacy by your cat, so you can see that the whole family will be happy to have you go through this extra process.

In the same way there is a trick to taking the forked bones out of a northern pike. Anybody who has eaten northern pike (or pickerel) knows that the forked bones are a problem. The flesh is delicious, but if you glom on to a mouthful of those forked bones you're likely to forgo the pleasure of eating the flesh for all time. They're not attached anywhere, and when they get in your mouth they seem to have a fiendish affinity for lodging at right angles to all the other forked bones.

It needn't be a problem. After the fish is cooked you can remove all these bones before you start eating. Then you have only the ribs and backbone, which are hooked together and easily removed, to contend with.

To do this, take the whole fish—or your piece of it, depending on whether it was baked whole or broiled or fried in chunks—and carefully open the shoulder about half an inch more or less (depending on the size of the fish) from the place where the back turns down and becomes the side. A fork is a good instrument to use for this.

If you see the single end of one of these forked bones, you have the right place. If you don't find it, try a little further down the side until you do; experiment. When you find a bone, open the piece of fish sideways in a line from that bone until you have the whole row of these bone-ends exposed the length of the fish or of your piece. Then just pull them out.

They go only as far back as the vent; the tail piece has only the backbone. But they are on both sides of the fish, so you have to go through the same process on the other side once you have finished the side you first started working on. After these bones are removed, eating the fish becomes a pleasure instead of a problem.

Lake Champlain sheepshead has a very bad reputation as an edible fish. To my way of thinking this is completely undeserved. It is a member of the drum family, and bears little resemblance to its striped salt-water namesake. On each side of its head inside its skull it has a "lucky stone." This is a round bone, unattached, which has on its face what a little imagination will convince you is a scroll *L*; or, if you pick up the other lucky stone and examine it first, a scroll *L* backwards. The scroll has enough resemblance to an *L* so you'll understand the origin of the name. You can have earrings made from the lucky stones, and other bits of costume jewelry.

The bad reputation as a table fish arises from efforts to cook sheepshead the way you'd cook other fish: by frying it or baking it or broiling it. If you do any of these it grows tougher the longer you cook it. If you continue to cook it with the idea that *more* cooking will tenderize it, boy, are you going to be surprised when you test it! It might make a good item for target practice with a .22 rifle. But you definitely aren't going to eat it short of a couple of damaged molars and a badly mutilated incisor.

Where, then, do I get the idea that its bad reputation is undeserved? Because, being a firm fish to start with, the way to cook it is to boil it. This would ruin most fish; they'd become a gooey mass. But boiling tenderizes sheepshead and yet lets it maintain its identity. Remove the slabs of flesh from the bones, serve with a cream gravy, and it is delicious. My father used to be very happy when we caught a sheepshead. We tried very hard for them.

I can remember a friend of mine telling me that he felt the way we did about sheepshead back when he was a boy, and had had a chance to get a big one from a man who had cheated him once in the past. My friend had just found a dead walleyed pike on the shore and was carrying it home to bury in the garden. The sharp dealer had just caught a large sheepshead.

When my friend appeared with the pike the man said, "I'd be willing to trade so you'd have the bigger fish. Just as a favor to you"—sort of smirking meanwhile because of the pike's good reputation and the sheepshead's bad one.

My friend said Sure; he'd trade. The trader didn't even know that he'd cheated himself until he tried to dress the pike and found he could stick a thumb into its side, it was so far gone.

The fact that boiled sheepshead tastes good is attested by the one area in which its eating reputation is excellent. It is considered by one and all a very fine chowder fish. And of course chowder fish is boiled. Where most fish go all to pieces, sheepshead does not disintegrate, and the fish chunks remain recognizable and are delicious.

In trolling we caught an occasional bass while the water was still murky early in our stay each year. About the first of August we had to change from silver trolling spoons to copper or brass, because the clearer water made the silver too bright except on a dark or rainy day. In August and on into September, we caught fewer and fewer northern pike, but those we did catch tended to be bigger and bigger.

My father's knowledge of how to troll for Lake Champlain pike was based on what *his* father had taught *him*. I was the third generation to fish that same area of lakeshore. My daughter came along and was the fourth generation. A fifth generation is summering in the area now.

In my grandfather's day you made your own trolling spoons out of—you guessed it—kitchen spoons that had a bent or broken handle, or which for some other reason could be talked out of the spoon drawer and into your tackle box. You straightened them, cut them, shaped them, fitted them with rings and swivels and hooks which you bought from the mail-order catalog. You tested them and re-tested them until you got them to perform when they were dragged under water, just exactly as you wanted them to.

When I first started to fish we had several of my grandfather's handmade trolling spoons, and these caught fish. Gradually, though, through the years we lost them to fish that broke our lines, until now there is just one left and I'm afraid to use that one lest I lose it.

In my father's day, manufactured trolling spoons were available, and after much trial and error we found that the kidney spinner, the fluted silver spinner, and the brass wobbler were the basic baits that were most likely to be successful. When the Dardevlet came along, we substituted that, in brass, for other brass wobblers.

We tried other baits, and at times they caught fish. One day we tried a tiny fluted brass spinner (the only one we had) as a last resort. It caught eight huge northern pike in half an hour, while the other outrigger caught nothing. One of the pike weighed eight and one-half pounds, another one weighed six. Of course we duplicated the spoon the first time we came near a store. And to this day neither that spoon nor the original has caught anything worth having.

Once we were landing to go for the milk and my father routinely said, "Okay, lift up your lines."

My mother, frustrated, said, "I won't." She left her line down, my father turned the boat toward shore. And just as the bow touched land, my mother got a huge strike.

Well, you can imagine the consternation that ensued. My father couldn't row anywhere—the bow was already touching the shore. He couldn't back; that would give the fish slack. Nobody could do anything constructive.

Yet somehow the fish stayed on and my mother brought him in. He weighed seven and one-quarter pounds. She couldn't even lift him with one hand. She had to hold him with one hand while she brought the other under his throat and lifted him two-handed. Of course we tried that maneuver a couple of times again— my father would do anything that would catch fish—and of course it never worked again.

Besides trolling and still-fishing, there were two legal techniques that were used once a year, a couple of weeks each. One—the one that is still used—was dragging for walleyed pike over the shallow spawning beds just south of where the broader lake begins, where the Champlain Bridge is now. You dragged very slowly with a sinker that bumped along the bottom and with a big gob of night crawlers on the hook. The season for this came (and still comes) a week or so each side of Memorial Day. On a day in the season, when the south wind blows strong and muddies the water, fishing is very productive.

And the other technique was used during the last weeks of August. It was called "riffling" for perch. Schools of perch drove schools of tiny transparent minnows to the surface and decimated them there, making the water boil for a few minutes. Then the school would disappear, and appear again near by when they caught up with the minnows once more. Following these schools and casting a worm into them was called riffling. It required a lot of rowing.

We used a small bamboo pole for this, with two baited hooks and no sinker, so that the baits would drift down through the school. You could catch more perch riffling than you ever could by still-fishing. But you needed a still day, both for the oarsman who had to back the boat in pursuit of the fish, and for the fishermen who had to see the riffle and direct the oarsman to it.

There hasn't been any really good riffling for twenty years or more. The perch still chase the transparent minnows at that time of year, the gulls scream and try to feed on the minnows or the perch or both. But the perch don't seem to follow the minnows and break water after them, a whole school of perch at a time, the way they used to. And for that reason they are nearly impossible to follow. Maybe the minnows have become less, maybe the perch have become less. The result is the same.

All in all, Lake Champlain fishing has always been a major attraction at the cottage. You had to like to fish. And you had to like to eat them. I have a feeling, on looking back over the years, that a person who didn't like to eat fish didn't come back and visit us a second time. His stomach rebelled. This was equally true when my father was running things, and later when I was in charge. Our coat of arms should have been a fish rampant on a bed of home-grown potatoes and vegetables.

6

Living Off the Land

It amuses me mildly, the idea that living off the land is something newly rediscovered after a lapse of several centuries, and that my generation was too busy making money to appreciate the simple pleasure of living from the bounty which Nature provides just for the taking.

I wish somebody would show me all this money my generation was too busy making. I must have been behind the door when it was being passed out. Or in the bathroom or some place. Most of my friends were in the same boat, and the boat was sinking. We'd scrape a few extra bucks together and Ol' Debbil Inflation would come along and club us right back to the same purchasing power we'd had before. Just like today.

In fact, it was because money was in such very short supply that we embraced wholeheartedly the simple pleasures of living off the land. Only we didn't call it "engaging in simple pleasures," we called it "trying to make both ends meet."

We wouldn't have understood refusing a good job, buying ten acres of land and an uninsulated old house, and retiring to it to work fourteen hours a day raising everything our family would get to eat—unless we had to. We would have understood (and most of us had to) living like that while we finished our education or waited for a new job to open up, or tried to make three dollars buy ten dollars worth of food after we'd been fired, or something like that. There was a depression back in the

Thirties that was a dilly-lou, but I for one knew all about living off the land long before that.

The cottage on Lake Champlain and the country surrounding it presented opportunities. We were there all summer. It's surprising what the combination of a big lake in rural surroundings, plenty of time, and a good deal of energy can produce. A lot of young people today would be amazed, maybe even flabbergasted, if they knew. I'm not sure exactly what "simple pleasures" means. But if it means we had one whale of a lot of fun doing these things, then it's right-on.

First there were those fish. We caught a lot of fish, both trolling and still-fishing—some of them big fish, as we've just seen. I pointed out that we liked fish and we didn't like walking ten miles round trip to the store for meat.

But in another way those fish helped us live off the land. When we caught more big northern pike than we could use (we'd throw the small ones back), we'd distribute them to our friends. You said you had a big northern pike you couldn't use, and would they have any use for one? If the Yes came with alacrity, even eagerness, you brought them another in a week or so. If it came hesitantly you brought them another in a month. If they asked who'd dress it, you dressed it for them and never gave them another, ever.

You very soon learned which families were eager to get fish and which families weren't. Remember that farm families, while they had horses and buggies and an occasional car for transportation, had the same basic problem we did in getting and keeping fresh meat in summer. Fish, just caught, was a welcome answer.

Now if you know Vermont farm families—or farm people anywhere—you know they don't intend to be "beholden" to anybody. It was true then even more than it is now, and it's plenty true now. So when we'd arrive with fish, they'd press upon us all sorts of *their* surplus. They had tremendous gardens. They had large stores of homemade jams and jellies. They had large flocks of chickens and hens, some of which weren't doing their part in egg production. Often one of these would end up on our table as fricasseed hen.

Important, but to a lesser degree, these farmers had areas near the barn which produced fishworms, which in turn produced perch and sheepshead and bass and mullet.

I'm afraid they didn't have to press very hard in trying to give us these things. We'd come away with maybe a bag of just-picked peas. If you've never eaten peas fresh-picked, you haven't lived gastronomically. A couple of days away from the garden and they're still good, but fresh-picked they're superb.

Or maybe in August it would be a supply of corn on the cob. They'd ask if we had time to wait while they went out and picked it. We did. Here again the shortness of time which elapses between garden and pot makes all the difference.

We ate string beans, turnips, beets, carrots, tomatoes, summer squash, cucumbers, to mention only the most likely gifts. In early summer we'd mostly get radishes and Swiss chard, but the choice would grow better all through the summer until, by the time we were ready to go back to Worcester, we'd be living off the fat of the land. The fish gifts also helped us get even for favors done us, like the use of the phone, the bringing of items from the store, and the like.

In addition to the largess of the neighbors, we had our own garden. We raised in it items that were scheduled to ripen in July and August (and the ones we were least likely to receive as gifts). This garden was on land where a cottage stands today.

The farmer on the farm which my father owned, would plow and harrow and plant the garden before we

64

arrived. When we did take up residence, the weed crop was unbelievable. My father—and I, most unwillingly—would spend several afternoons with hoes doing-in the weeds so that the vegetables could flourish. Then would begin our fish treatment.

We dressed a lot of fish in the course of the summer, and we would bury the heads and the entrails next to the hills of corn and potatoes and squash and cucumbers, and later beside the rows where we had row-crops. There was also a sucker-type fish called a mullet which we caught while we were still-fishing for perch, which had more bones than a pincushion has pins, and these we'd chop in half and bury too. Shortly after the fish treatment, the plants would perk up amazingly, and for those that could really get their roots into the mullet halves, the result would be astounding: big dark green plant foliage and lush produce.

Maybe, though, I make it sound easier than it was. Because the skunks and raccoons would promptly dig up at night any fish you buried in the daytime. Furthermore, if you had done the burying too close to young plants, they would become casualties of the digging-up process.

The way to handle this problem was with saturation burying. Every day we'd re-bury what had been dug up, and add new burials. The trick was to bury the fish at just the right distance from the plants—not too far to do any good, not so near that the plants would be dug up as well. Too often we failed in this attempt.

But as we got more and more fish buried at more and more places, ideally all over the garden, the animals would find they had more work cut out for them than they could do in one night. Thus they'd stick pretty much to the newer, juicier burial spots and leave alone, or give just a token scratching to, the older re-burials.

Their nighttime working hours were further cut into, judging from night shrieks in the garden, indicating jurisdictional disputes. If you think for a minute the animals were able to find the buried fish only because we didn't hide the signs of digging, boy, are you naïve. The nose of a coon or a skunk *knows* what's been buried. I once buried some fish, then built a fire on the place, and that night it was dug up. And if you think they find fish easily, try burying chicken bones sometime and see how fast *those* are found.

But on the whole the fish treatment was effective, and after the plant roots had grown out into the fish, the results were spectacular.

The eating was just as spectacular when the garden began to produce. In addition to the garden we had two cherry trees which the robins and the Hoyts fought over, with the crop divided about 50–50 between the contestants. We had currant bushes (this was before anybody knew they were an intermediate host to the insect that causes white-pine blister) and blackberry and raspberry bushes.

These were ours. But for the taking, in the public domain, were other delicacies. Most notable among them were the wild strawberries. They're much smaller, sweeter and juicier than tame berries. They're just plain delicious.

In case you've never picked them, they grow mostly on worn-out land that hasn't seen a plow for some time. There's less and less of this kind of land each year, but at that time there was plenty. You took medium-sized pans, and a couple of members of the family to help, and you went into one of these fields within easy walking distance of the cottage. You picked the stems, and each stem had three, four, or maybe five berries on it. The good picking was in patches. When one of the party found such a productive patch the others would join in covering it completely. When it had been pretty thoroughly covered, somebody would wander on looking for another patch.

When your pans were heaping you returned home and picked-over the berries. You found, when you

66

started this, that your work had actually just begun, and that this second part was drudgery compared to the first. You'd be lucky if you didn't finish the chore with stiff and aching arms and back.

But it was worth the work, believe me. Many's the time I've sat down to a supper of wild strawberry shortcake and nothing else. The season for wild berries was, and is, comparatively short, and it behooves you to make the most of it.

After wild strawberries, the wild raspberries and blackcaps would come along. Our cultivated berries were bigger and darker, but there weren't enough of them to satisfy us. And in the wooded areas near by, and along the roadsides, were patches of wild raspberry bushes. You went to these each day during the bearing season, and kept them picked clean. There was a good bit of secrecy about where these patches were located, and to reach the ones you had discovered you walked via the lakeshore or by some other roundabout route calculated to keep you from being seen. Actually, your only competition was the farmers' wives and kids of the area, and at that time of year, when the husbands were haying, they were busy too.

These berries also were used for shortcakes. And whereas I liked them a lot, they never came close to wild strawberries for flavor. However, we sure picked and ate an awful lot of raspberries and blackcaps.

Blackberries came next. These also grew in lightly wooded areas, along roadsides, at the edge of brush heaps, in clearings where there would be sunlight. They were likely to be big and juicy and tasty, but they are a berry which has a lot of small hard seeds with an affinity for lodging themselves between your teeth. Some people avoid blackberries for that reason.

We might have ignored them too, except that they came along late in the summer, well after the other berries were gone, and it was them or nothing. It was unthinkable that, with a berry so big and beautiful, the answer should be nothing.

There were no blueberries near us. They grew in the foothills of the Green Mountains of Vermont or the Adirondacks of New York. The Green Mountains were much too far away to hike to and still have any time left in the day for berry-picking. But the Adirondack foothills were only about three and a half miles away, directly across the lake. There was another three and a half miles to the top of the first mountain.

So, once each summer, when Uncle Fred and Uncle Harry were at the cottage with us, we'd take the skiff, row across the lake, and climb Bald Peak. It was no mean climb, but the view in all directions from the top was stupendous. A couple of times we camped out overnight at the top.

From there everything looked tiny: toy houses and farms, toy boats on Champlain. Even the steamship *Vermont* looked like a toy, her wake spread like a peacock tail behind her. On a clear day you could see into Canada and as far as Mount Washington in the White Mountains of New Hampshire. Below us on the Vermont side of the lake we could pick out our cottage, Loomis's orchard, Vergennes, Addison, the Champlain Memorial, the Narrows, and Split Rock Mountain.

Always when we climbed "Baldy" we would carry our food in pails. And once it was eaten we'd fill the pails with blueberries. There were in those days vast quantities of them at the top of the mountain. And since New Yorkers could find good berry patches much nearer home, wild horses couldn't have dragged them up that tough old mountain to get the ones we were after. Thus our only competition was the hikers who came up for the view, and they didn't eat many and carried home even less.

Once we got the blueberries home we'd use them in shortcake, muffins, tarts, pie and of course plain with cream. You name it, we ate it. Even then it was touch-and-go whether we could successfully refrigerate the dwindling supply of berries until they were all gone. Nowadays you'd simply freeze your surplus; we couldn't do that in those days. But we made out pretty well. Still, for a week or so after the berries were all gone you had a feeling you were spitting blue, and your toothbrush seemed to have a definite bluish tinge.

I have, though, a warm spot in my heart for those blueberries; the ones atop old Baldy were big and juicy, and I can still remember the taste of them. Probably the blueberry supply up there has dwindled by now. Through field glasses it looks as if brush and small trees have grown up all around the mountain's bald spot, and this would cut down on the sunlight. When we used to go there the mountain was getting over a forest fire which had pretty thoroughly denuded the whole top area. Evidently there's been no fire in recent times.

Two perennial spring and early summer food sources which most country-dwellers in my youth availed themselves of, took up very little room. They were the asparagus bed and rhubarb patch. Those two items furnished the most nourishment from the least space, of anything I know about. Some farm families had no more asparagus than two huge clumps, one on each side of the back steps. And yet they got fine meals of asparagus in the early spring. Furthermore, when the plants were allowed to grow up and go to seed in late June, they furnished a very ornamental planting for the steps or yard.

We arrived at the cottage too late for asparagus. But we enjoyed a whole lot of rhubarb pies and many dishes of rhubarb sauce. A set of farm buildings had burned near us and the rhubarb and asparagus beds, one apple tree, and the cellarhole were all that was left. My father asked and received permission to keep the rhubarb bed in good shape in return for rhubarb to eat.

All these expeditions and this garden work took time. But we *had* time. We had *lots* of time. It was fun, and it gave you a terrifically pleasant feeling of accomplishment, of "providing."

Along about the first of August the fruit of an early apple tree down at the farm would be pronounced ripe and ready for pie-making. We'd go down and pick one or two apples.

I know that sounds crazy, but I mean exactly that. Because this was an apple tree to end all apple trees. Each apple was immense, easily twice or three times the size of an ordinary apple. They were so sour they'd screw your mouth all up, and they'd rot before they'd get any other way. But with plenty of sugar in your pie, Presto! the apple taste would come to the fore and you had a terrific pie. Oh, you'd get better pies when the main apple crop came on in September, but this was about the first of August, remember.

The tree is gone now. It went, and my father died, before I had a chance to learn what it was. I've since looked in fruit-tree books and it might be one of several varieties of giant early apples. My father told me at the time, but I can't recall the name now. I am indebted to that tree, though, for some fine summer pie-eating. In addition to everything else, its branches grew in such a way that it was easy for a boy to climb—which, when you are a boy, is a desirable attribute in any tree.

We had another source of considerable nourishment. We used to collect meadow mushrooms, an act which used to make everybody, especially the farm community, aghast. I've eaten an awful lot of meadow mushrooms in my time; they're terrific eating if you stick to the young buttons. I'm no mushroom buff. Some people know dozens of varieties that are edible. I know just one, and I stick strictly to that one which I am sure of. I also know the "Death Angels" and am thus doubly able to avoid *them*.

Pastures were the best place to find mushrooms when we were at the cottage in late August. A golf course is your best bet now, though. The live-off-the-land set know about mushrooms. We used to be the only eaters of wild mushrooms around, but today their number is legion. Most of them are real buffs too, comparing learnedly the flavor of one variety with another. They have a tendency to look the length of the nose at my utilitarian, one-variety identification system.

Several times we managed fall-foliage trips to the cottage which took advantage of the October 12th holiday. And when we did, we gathered as large a supply as we could of hickory nuts for the next summer's cooking and eating.

My father's boyhood in the area stood us in good stead: he knew which trees bore prodigiously, which ones grew nuts that cracked well, which ones shed their outer husk when they dropped, which ones produced the biggest nuts. He also knew which trees to avoid because their product behaved poorly in these matters.

Nowadays hickory nuts are not highly thought of, although their flavor is delicate and delicious. But they are very hard to crack and harder still to pick out. Most people won't go to that much trouble when packaged nutmeats are so easy to pick up in the store.

But we used to count ourselves lucky to get them. And for those who have never been introduced to the art of cracking them, there is just one thing to know. If you hold them on edge and crack them on that narrow edge, a great many of the halves will come out intact, thus making the picking-out easier. By hitting them on that narrow edge, the cheeks of the shell will break away and the meat will stand exposed. It's as simple as that.

If you lay them flat and hit them on the side, they'll shatter and the picking-out will be an impossible task. Use a hammer or a nutcracker; it makes little difference. The important thing is cracking them on edge. A

71

hickory-nut pie, using the recipe for pecan pie with hickory nuts instead of pecan meats, is a gourmet's delight.

Butternuts, which we sometimes got and which are even harder to crack, must be cracked on the *end* for good results.

In non-food items, we used to gather sassafras roots from a swampy area for a tea which my grandmother used to swear by. And we collected thoroughwort which was made into a tonic which produced perspiration in the person who drank it. The only thing I remember about thoroughwort is that the leaves were double and the stalk grew up through them instead of the leaves being attached to the stalk.

I have mentioned the driftwood we gathered, and how we brought it home in the skiff. This was another non-food item. Burned in the fireplace on cool evenings, it furnished all the heat we needed during the summer months when we were at the cottage.

There were in those days almost unlimited amounts of this driftwood available for the taking. Our part of Lake Champlain is an area of clay banks with now and then a gully where the runoff from the fields enters the lake. At high-water time the water in these gullies widens out and extends back into the fields. Driftwood bumps along the steep bank where there is no resting place for it, until it reaches one of the gullies. The wind drives it inside these little coves, and, since there is nothing to drive it out again, it remains there. The water recedes and leaves it there. It's high, and though it isn't dry then, it gets dry very soon.

By the time we'd arrive at the cottage in late June it was dry and ready to burn. And there were so many of these wood-filled gullies within rowing distance that we'd be awfully choosy.

If a piece of wood wasn't perfect, we'd leave it. If it needed to be chopped for any reason, we'd leave it. If it needed to be split, the heck with it. With so many perfect pieces just the right size for our fireplace, why lug home stuff that had to be worked on? Nowadays when I am lucky enough to find a supply of driftwood, all of which has to be worked over, I remember those days with longing.

The lake's waters brought us other things through the years. One such item was a deck chair from one of the old lake steamers. It was a chair which some gentleman in his cups had probably been unable to unfold and in a fit of pique had rid himself of. We kept and used the chair for years. Once we came upon more than a dozen oranges within a short stretch of shoreline, with which we could find nothing wrong. We ate them and they were delicious. Another time we rescued an old tub of a boat which was drifting past. We pulled it up on our shore and waited for the owner to come for it, which he never did. We made inquiries, found nothing. Finally at the end of the season we sold the thing for five dollars. Once a very nice boathook drifted in. We didn't have much use for a boathook; it stayed around four or five years and then I lost track of it.

As I grew older the inclination and need to live off the land did not diminish. I quit my coaching job four years out of college to work full time as a free-lance writer. And when editors were unkind for any extended length of time, that was when I really needed to live off the land. Add the fact that two years later I took unto myself a wife, and you get the picture.

The summer we were married I spent a lot of spare time at the cottage before the wedding, putting in the garden personally. And after the wedding we came to Vermont and lived at the cottage. We fished and bartered fish, we did all the things I have described. That fall we picked up drop McIntosh apples at fifty cents a bushel at Loomis's orchard, and canned a lot of them into applesauce.

We canned other things, too, from the garden. And when late fall came we packed the cans twenty-four to a case, in eight cases, put them in our Whippet car, and went to spend the winter in Florida on the Gulf of Mexico. There we ate quantities of saltwater fish and filled our canning jars, as fast as we emptied them, with drop grapefruit sections to eat the next summer—grapefruit which we were allowed to pick up in a grove for twenty-five cents a bushel.

There's something basic about living off the land which is extremely satisfying. Each generation that comes along thinks they discovered it, and probably those that follow us will too. Living off the land will be different then, just as it was different in my time from the generation before me. More people, less wild space, make the change.

But in my time, sometimes through sheer necessity, I got to be quite an expert.

7

Bee Hunting

When we hadn't anything else to do on a sunny warm summer afternoon, we'd go bee-hunting.

Bee-hunting was a food sport from my father's boyhood. He had the necessary bee box left over from those times. He taught me to use it, and I was excited by bee-hunting and loved it right from the start.

Briefly, a colony of bees "swarms" at least once a year. After making sure there is a supply of new queens in the larva stage—one of whom will kill the others and reign as queen of the old hive—the old queen takes about half the worker bees and goes out to set up a new colony.

Nowadays when beekeeping is a full-time occupation, the swarming bees are "hived" by the owner and he has a new colony. He makes available a box-hive with frames full of empty wax cells and has it waiting for the bees to move into and there they go right to work. It is a far better, more convenient home than they could find anywhere in the wild. And they embrace their opportunity.

But when I was a boy, a farmer who raised bees had up to fifteen or twenty hives as a strict sideline, since he spent most of his time farming his fields. He might not notice the signs which told that a colony was thinking of swarming, and they'd get away. When they did that, they'd pick a hollow tree and set up housekeeping there.

It was these tree-housed colonies that bee-hunting was designed to find.

The bee box that I spoke of, and which we used to hunt bee trees, had a sliding cover. You placed a little dish of comb honey inside on the box's bottom. We used an antique salt dish. In the sliding cover there was a tiny rectangle of glass, and this too had a sliding cover.

You approached a bee on a flower, held the box under the flower, and gently knocked the bee into the box. At the same instant with your index finger you slid the cover shut.

The bee buzzed in there angrily. But fairly soon it discovered the honey and stopped buzzing and started to fill its honey stomach. You then slid back the cover over the glass insert. If the bee flew to the light, you closed out the light again. If it didn't, you placed the box atop a fencepost or stump and carefully slid the main cover open half an inch or so.

We'll say there were three of you hunting. Each of you took up a position low to the ground from which you could see the bee box against the sky. You'd probably divide the circle around the bee box roughly in thirds, but the decisive factor in choosing your spot would be the amount of cleared space to see the bee against the sky no matter in what direction it flew.

Then you'd wait for the bee to finish filling itself with honey and come out.

This it would do, probably about the time you decided something must be the matter and were starting forward to find out what the trouble was.

The bee would hover around the opening a few moments. Then it would move away a few feet, make a half-circle, return, make another part-circle, each one wider and a little higher than the one before.

You've heard that "a bee circles, and then goes to its hive in a straight line." This is not true. There seems to be no rhyme or reason to the figure eights, part-circles, half-circles, the bee makes in fixing the area in its mind. And when it starts for the hive it flies in a wavering line, and it doubles back one or more times clear to the bee box. About the best you can say for the "beeline" is that it's in the direction of the hive, but not in a straight line toward it.

If the three hunters were on the ball and had reasonably good eyesight, they'd be able to decide among them the theoretical straight line which came nearest the middle of the wavering course the bee took.

You would draw, then, a rough map of the area and you would plot that line-of-flight on it. If the line-of-flight went toward an apiary (and maybe 95 percent of them do) you would charge that bee off to profit and loss, take up your bee box and go get another bee. You'd start the new bee off from a fencepost considerably removed from the one you used first.

But if the line-of-flight went in any other direction than toward an apiary, adrenalin would start to flow: you might have a live one.

You'd wait. And wait. And wait. Suddenly a bee

would re-appear, hovering above the opening in the bee box. It would hover momentarily, drop inside. Maybe there would be several bees if their home happened to be close to the place where you were working. The first bee would have told others in the colony, by an almost unbelievable system of bee communication, where it found its honey.

You'd watch and line up the bee when it left, line up the others that arrived. Others would "tell" others. Pretty soon you'd have four or five bees in the box at a time.

When you had several bees in the box at one time you'd slip near and close the cover of the box. You'd take up the box, leaving in its place a small square of comb honey on the fencepost to maintain the line you had already established in case you later needed it. Then with the box you'd move as rapidly as possible at right angles to the line the bees had taken.

You'd go a considerable distance in that direction, maybe even as much as one-eighth of a mile. You'd pick another fencepost or stump, set the box on it and slide the cover open a little.

The bees would come out angrily, buzz around furiously for a moment or two. But then they'd calm down and go into the half-circle-figure-eight bit until they had memorized this new location. Then they'd waver off in a new beeline.

And after you and your fellow hunters were sure of the line, you'd draw it on your rough map. Where this new line crossed the old one, the bee tree would be located.

You'd wait until you had bees back in the box again. Then you'd close the box and carry it to the spot where the lines came together. There again you'd release the bees, establish a third line, this time very close to the tree.

You'd leave the box where it was and begin to look up into the trees as near the junction of the lines as you could figure that junction to be. You'd try to see every knothole on every tree against the sky to determine if a line of bees was passing in and out of an opening.

You might have to move the box once more, but sooner or later you would find the tree. And that is always a great feeling of triumph.

Usually you'd wait a year before "taking up" the bee tree. This is not a sport for the impatient. The theory is that if the bees haven't stored enough honey to winter the colony, it wouldn't have been worth your labor to cut the tree.

If, however, the bees are still there the next summer, you'd see the owner of the land, explain what you wanted to do and get his permission. Usually he'd give you permission if you promised to cut and split up the wood for him when you were finished.

When we hunted bees at the cottage there was a law on the books that gave you the right to cut a bee tree if you paid the owner the value of the tree. This would not be much because the tree of necessity has to be a hollow tree and so is worth nothing for lumber. By being co-operative you can usually work out the matter with the owner. It's a pretty good idea not to divulge the exact location of the bee tree until you are sure the right to cut it has been granted.

When you have permission, you get together your equipment. You'll need an efficient saw. We used a two-man crosscut; nowadays you'd probably use a chain saw. You'll also need a beekeeper's veil for each worker, and a beekeeper's smoker, along with a pair of leather gloves, heavy overalls over your regular pants, and a heavy jacket. These items are for your protection. The sleeves of your jacket should be tied at the wrist and your pants at the ankles to keep bees from crawling up inside. You need a sledgehammer and wedges. The smoker quiets the bees: instinct tells them, when they smell smoke, that their home is endangered by fire and they begin to fill their honey stomachs with the colony's stores to remove to a new location. If they're doing this they can't be attacking you.

You should get a beekeeper to furnish you an unoccupied hive which you set near the tree. This should be equipped with empty combs all ready for a new colony, the one that's now in the tree you're going to cut. You promise, in return, to try to hive the bees for his apiary.

Then you cut the tree, trying to make it land in such a way that the honeycombs will be damaged as little as possible by the fall.

Once the tree is on the ground, use the smoker on the bees' entrance hole. Then cut into the log six or eight feet each side of the hole. If your saw teeth show honey, stop at once and move further from the hole. Split the hollow log with the wedges and the sledgehammer when you cut it away from the rest of the trunk. It will open up and the long combs (looking nothing like the square commercial combs) will lie exposed in front of you.

These combs are made up of the same-sized hexagonal wax cells that you'd find in a commercial hive. How the little engineers get every one of these hexagons the same size, how they know that the hexagon is the only shape that would utilize every infinitesimal bit of space by fitting exactly against every other hexagon, nobody will ever know.

The feat is more amazing when you understand that each cell is worked on by hundreds of bees. Flakes of wax are produced between the middle segments of the underside of the bee, are scraped off with the legs and transferred to the mandibles, are chewed into a soft little ball and carried under the chin to the place where the work of cell-building is going on.

There the bee adds his little glob of wax to the work, shapes it, draws it out very thin indeed. Yet with all these different bees working on the project, each cell always ends up the same as every other, and each comb is just

the right distance from every other comb when capped, so that bees can pass between the combs freely and work.

In a hive, the comb is fitted into the rectangular frames furnished by the beekeeper. In a bee tree, where the space is long and round, the combs are some of them many feet long. And yet, even though they are that long and the weight of such a long comb full of honey is very great, some bee engineer makes the wax—which bonds them to the tree at the top and sides—thick enough and strong enough so that they never break away.

These long combs, some of them badly smashed by the tree's fall, are your spoils. You gather up these spoils in kettles, dishpans, anything suitable that doesn't leak, which you have brought for the purpose.

In collecting the honey, keep looking for a bee about one-third again as long as a regular honeybee; this will be the queen. She will have a lot of workers around her. If you see her, stop what you are doing and take her to the new hive and put her inside.

Whether you see the queen or not, cut all large pieces of the brood (the unhatched eggs, larvae, unborn bees in their wax cells) from the combs you are taking, and put this brood into the new hive to hatch out there.

Usually after the bees get over the first shock they will find the queen if you haven't, and will rally to her and hang in a big festoon from the place she has chosen to light, just the way they do when they are swarming. Their scouts will find the hive you have left for them and the colony will move in. The beekeeper will have to feed them some, come winter, but he will get a good colony.

You won't be able to use for the table the comb honey you have taken, because it was probably messed up and crushed too much in the tree's fall. It will have to be strained through cheesecloth.

In commercial honey you can tell by the flavor what flowers the honey was made from. But you can't tell with wild honey, which has a strong taste from so much pollen, brood and beebread mixed in. Beebread is the pollen-based material that is fed to the larvae. All the wild honey I've ever eaten has this strong taste. But it is sweet and good. It can be used as a spread for toast, a sweetener for coffee or cereal, or mixed with something else as a filling for sandwiches. It can be served with biscuits or muffins just like any honey.

It can be used in cooking. But if you use it in cooking there are certain differences between honey and sugar which you have to bear in mind. Honey is 17 percent water, and is sweeter, cup for cup, than sugar. In making bread you use three-fourths of a cup of honey to replace each one cup of sugar. And some cooks feel you should cut the amount of milk the recipe calls for to make up for the 17 percent of water the honey contains. Don't cut it much; some bakers don't cut it at all, claiming that to do so makes the bread or cake crumble.

Some bakers have concluded that it is never wise to substitute honey for more than half the sugar in sweetening. They claim that to bake entirely with honey causes the product to take on a sogginess that is unpleasant. One thing especially advantageous about baking with honey is that the qualities in honey, notably the extra moisture, cause the product to remain moist and stay fresh longer than ordinary baked goods.

But getting back to bee-hunting, is there any way you can take up a bee tree without felling it? There never was when I was hunting bees at the cottage. But with the advent of the chain saw some people claim that it can be done. You cut a rectangular piece out of the back of the trunk of your bee tree with the oval end of the chain saw, rob the tree of some of its better combs, and then wire the rectangular piece back in place. Hopefully you can remove it and open the tree again the next year.

This would have the tremendous advantage of not damaging the combs in the crash of the tree. And of course would give you what amounted to a domestic hive. It could be harvested year after year, and could even be fed and serviced like an apiary hive to the advantage of both bees and owner.

Why don't bears rob bee trees in the wild and wooded areas? Well, it's because the bees have thought of this, and usually pick an opening too high for bears to attack while they are still standing on solid ground. A bear is not at his best trying to rob a colony with one paw, while he clings to the trunk of the tree with the other three.

Bears do occasionally rob bee trees. They tear at the opening with their teeth and try to enlarge it enough so they can reach a paw inside. In doing this they get stung brutally around the nose and the eyes and away from the thick mat of hair. They whimper and yelp in pain, but they keep on trying.

Mostly they don't succeed; the wood is too hard and thick and the position too awkward. Add to this the fact that they have to keep their eyes closed to avoid being stung in the eyeballs, and you have some idea of the poor working conditions under which they operate. A bear has a far, far easier time with a manmade hive which he can demolish with one swipe of his paw, thus spreading its goodies on the ground there in front of him. He still gets stung, but not the way he does in robbing, or trying to rob, a bee tree.

When I was very young I helped take up a bee tree from which we got four quarts of strained honey, an unusually small amount. I insisted on carrying the quart jars home to Worcester in my suitcase—they just about filled it—and my clothes and possessions had to get home some other way.

We usually had two, three, or four bee trees that we were "wintering" and most of these colonies would die out over the winter. But when you *did* take up a tree that had wintered, you might get sixty or even a hundred pounds of honey if the tree was big and the colony had been there a long while. Until just a year or so ago there was a bee tree right in a shade-tree maple in front of the old town hall building in Vergennes, ten or twelve feet above the sidewalk. It was a shade-tree maple, and it was there as long back as I can remember. I always thought it was safe from being cut down because of the dim view the city fathers would take toward the removal of a shade tree, to say nothing of the tearing down of overheard wires, the blocking of Main Street, the damaging of the street and sidewalk, and the stinging of every innocent person who moved in the area without being protected. But I think it was sometime during the summer of 1973 that the city crew took it down.

So now you know how we used to get our sweets from the land. If we'd been at the cottage in early spring I'm sure we'd have boiled maple sap and enjoyed maple syrup and maple sugar, because we had a considerable grove of hard maples at the farm.

I wonder if young people today ever do anything with bee-hunting. I haven't seen any signs of it in my area in a number of years. Certainly it was a fun way to produce the winter's supply of sweets. And once you tasted wild honey you'd never forget it. For a steady diet I'd choose apiary honey. But I'd like a chance at some wild honey now and then just for variety, even today.

8

The Visit of Troop 24

It is impossible to stress enough the impact that the cottage on Lake Champlain had on my life and, I'm sure, on my character.

I spent roughly one-sixth of my early life in and around the cottage, the most impressionable years of all. A city boy, I learned about the water, the woods, fish, wildlife, farming, farm animals, open fields. When I returned to Worcester each fall and walked up the walk to our home on the Clark University campus (there are no houses there now; they've all been torn down) the grounds which had seemed rather vast to me two months earlier, seemed small and cramped after my sojourn among wide fields. The buildings seemed to have been moved much closer together.

I gained skills which a city boy seldom gains. I learned to catch fish, to dress them, to hoe various crops, to drive horses. I learned how to recognize poison ivy and avoid it, how to avoid being stung by hornets. Above all I learned the water skills—how to swim and dive, how to row a boat, how to paddle a canoe. Plus the important refinement for a round-bottomed boat: how to spread your feet wide when rowing in the trough of the waves, and flip the gunwale up a little as the wave-crest reached you. This required an infinite amount of practice.

Also something else that required a lot of practice was rowing when the oars were not attached to the oarlocks. Even today I don't consciously think about holding the oars centered; I just row and the oars never slide in or out in the oarlocks, thanks to the skill I developed as a boy. And there was the ability to paddle stern in a canoe with the paddle at an angle so the canoe would travel in a straight line. The variations you had to make were made automatically, without thought, by changing minutely the angle at which you held the paddle. This allowed you to stroke in continuous rhythm with the bow paddler without losing strokes or rhythm for steering.

As I've said, I loved the life at the cottage, longed for it all year, grew increasingly excited as the time to go there approached, grew morose and teary as the time approached to leave. And I wanted my friends to share what I enjoyed so much.

I never thought about it in just that way, but that was what it amounted to. And in looking back on it, I think subconsciously I wanted to enjoy my experiences all over again by watching my friends experience and enjoy them.

Accordingly, my family and I reached a compromise. I could invite one friend at a time to the cottage for not longer than a month. Among the ones I invited were Sid Gage (many times), Bob Mooney, Bud Sampson, Earnie Doty, Chet Ricker, Al Brason.

Each had a lot of adventures. Al Brason ran afoul of a hornets' nest. Bud Sampson came upon a litter of baby skunks too small, in his estimation, to understand about spraying as a means of protecting themselves; Bud's error in judgment meant that we had to bury his camp clothes and scour him with an abrasive soap.

My father forgot to hand Bob Mooney his ticket when he got on the train at Vergennes to return home. There was then much telegraphing back and forth to stations between Vergennes and Rutland trying to undo this tragedy of a lone small boy on board a train without a ticket or much of any money. Later we found that a

Vergennes businessman, a friend of my father's, had seen Bob with us at the station. When he overheard the problem as the conductor collected tickets, he came to the rescue and advanced the money for Bob's passage. For years afterward I had a warm spot in my heart for Mr. Herrick, the man who had done this.

In addition to those of my friends who visited us at the cottage there was one, Gus Dann, who got a job, through my father's efforts, at the Pratt farm across the bay from the cottage during the "Work-on-a-Farm" program of World War I. Gus was older than I was, but I saw him often that summer and fished with him some during his time off.

However, the one-boy-one-month edict didn't satisfy me completely. It left too many of my friends and acquaintances with no knowledge whatever of the marvelous place I spent the summer. They had no firsthand knowledge of the good times available. Like all zealots, I believed so wholeheartedly in this one thing that I wanted a chance to convert everybody.

I knew better than to make a frontal attack on the rule, but I applied pressure wherever and whenever the opportunity presented itself, and as much as my instinct told me was safe.

As a result of this oblique pressure I finally received permission to spend Easter vacation at the cottage with three of my pals—just the four of us with no adults. I suspect, looking back on it, that my parents had long, long thoughts about this, and many a serious family council after I'd gone to bed at night. But the permission was forthcoming. The rule still stood for the summer when the family was in residence, but this exception seemed reasonable for a one-week, non-adult camping trip.

I picked three companions from my Boy Scout troop, because cooking and camping skills were essential. Two were Eagle Scouts, Chet Ricker and Brad Reed; I was a Life Scout, and Jack Hodgson was a First Class Scout. It was also necessary that their families have money enough to stand the railroad fare from Worcester to Lake Champlain.

It was a real adventure for all of us. Chet was in charge. We all had daily assignments. We had a boat and fished, and we rowed to various places, like the old forts and Port Henry. We hiked, visited the farm. We even swam—once—though the ice had been gone from the lake only a matter of days. We swam that once so we could say we had, and so we could have a picture taken to prove it. But it was an emotional experience. I have been in cold water since, but nothing that even remotely approached that water. It took your breath away. It bugged your eyes out.

The day was unusually warm for that time of year. The water was very high, what with the spring runoff, and you could dive from the big rock at the top of the beach, a rock which was completely out of water in summer.

Jack was the first one in. He looked so horrified that I started to laugh. But Jack put his forefinger to his lips and I shut up. Brad Reed had his back turned and was getting out of his pants.

He called, "How is it?"

And Jack said, "Surprisingly warm. Very pleasant." He wasted no time in getting out, though.

Brad's natural caution thus allayed, he stepped onto the rock and balanced there. Then he dove in.

I have never seen anything like that since: his feet seemed to be still entering the water as the front end of him burst out. And he had somehow turned under water and was facing us when his head re-appeared. His eyes stuck out; you could have hung things on them. His mouth was wide open but no sound came from it. He surged toward shore and a noise like a death rattle finally made it from between his open lips.

His surging was aimed toward Jack, and Jack got the message. He started up out of there and Brad was only a few steps behind him. Chet and I watched. It was pretty interesting, really. It was the only time I ever saw two barefoot boys, stark naked and in broad daylight, running off across the fields, one of them having trouble because he was laughing so hard.

The hiking, you would have expected us to do. But the thing you would never have expected was that we would spend all our spare time, those idle minutes when we didn't have anything big afoot, playing cricket. That's what I said: cricket. Only one of us had ever played it before, but the game lent itself admirably to our make-shift equipment and the shape of the playing area available to us. We used an old tennis ball in place of a cricket ball, and the blade of a broken oar for a cricket bat, and a propped-up board for a wicket.

And we had fun. Obviously cricket played with two on a side required certain modifications; these we agreed on. We played off and on for a whole week. I've never played the game since, have seen only one contest in my life and that was at Haverford College. But that week it filled the bill admirably.

My father arrived at the end of our stay to make sure the cottage was closed well and things were taken care of the way he wanted them to be. He had been at Dartmouth to judge a debate, and instead of going directly home had come around by way of Vergennes. I later saw a letter he wrote my mother in which he mentioned that we didn't keep dishes, utensils, stove and kitchen as clean as she would have. And that on the train trip home "they raised cain, but nothing serious."

All in all, though, we had some fine meals and were still all speaking to each other at the end of the week.

We were glad to see my father when he arrived. He was our scoutmaster at home and had been for years. And I was glad on the further count that he was my father. Incidentally, many years later on my wedding day, Chet Ricker received his announcement of that event, put it in his pocket, and with his wife got into their car and headed for the cottage to spend the first week of our honeymoon with us.

In June, shortly after returning from our four-boy camping trip, one of the great tragedies of my life occurred. My father, who had been having angina pains and hadn't said much about them, had an attack one Saturday afternoon while he was watching his scouts play a baseball game against another troop. I was at bat in one of the middle innings when they came and took me to him. He died within a few minutes after I got there.

I had been very close to my father, and his death engulfed me. My world was shattered. I could not imagine the cottage, my home, anything else without him. It was a horrible time. It has, in later years, been very saddening to know that if the nitroglycerin method of treating angina had been perfected then to the extent it is today, he would have had the tablets with him and might reasonably have lived many, many more years.

So that spring I made another and very sorrowful trip to West Addison, where I had been so recently and so happily. Lake View Cemetery looks down across sloping fields and pastures to Lake Champlain and the Adirondacks beyond. From where I stood when they lowered my father's body I could see the cottage to the north on the lakeshore. It was the place where we had enjoyed each other so much. That moment was one of the worst I have ever had to live through.

That summer the ache that was with me all the time began to dull somewhat, as it is bound to do. And probably because of the huge vacancy that had suddenly developed in my life, I turned more than ever to my friends to fill it. More than ever I wanted *all* my friends to see, live at, and enjoy the cottage on Lake Champlain.

Taking three boys there in spring vacation, instead

of just one at a time, had been a big step in the right direction. I suppose I would ordinarily have been satisfied with that. Some of us, especially the four who had been there together, talked idly from time to time about taking the whole scout troop up there for the same sort of camping experience we had enjoyed. But it was only talk; only a few in the troop had that kind of money.

After my father's death, Jack Hodgson's father took over as scoutmaster of Troop 24. Mr. Hodgson owned Queensbury Knitting Mills there in Worcester. In turn, the knitting mills owned trucks. They were very different from modern trucks. They were very slow, and had a chain drive and solid rubber tires. But they were very elegant and the last word in transportation at that time.

One day when we were talking about a trip to the lake, Jack said, "Maybe Dad would furnish one of the mill trucks." And that was the beginning of the idea. Jack worked on his father, I worked on my mother. And very slowly the trip began to jell.

As the time for the start approached there was much planning in Worcester. Lists of boys were made, parental approval was obtained. Tents were borrowed, lists of equipment and supplies re-checked.

At the cottage, meanwhile, my mother and I had done what we could to make ready for the scouts' arrival. I had rented four boats and rowed each one of them to the cottage, and with our two I felt they would do us very nicely. The last week before the scheduled arrival, a woman asked my mother to do something and Mother said, "I'm sorry, I can't. I've invited a large troop of boy scouts to spend a couple of weeks with us." The woman's face was absolutely horrified.

Finally, on August 17, 1921, at 5:30 A.M., the big red truck left Worcester. It was a $3\frac{1}{2}$-ton Stewart (not many people today have ever heard of a Stewart, let alone seen one). It carried the tents, the food, and the boys. A long cloth sign, stretching the length of the truck on each side,

said WORCESTER TO LAKE CHAMPLAIN. B.S.A. TROOP 24.
There were twenty-six boys. Two more, Bud Hutchins
and I, would join the expedition when it reached the
cottage. Mr. Hodgson and his brother-in-law, Mr. Albee,
were in charge. Ed Wild was the truck driver and a better
choice could not have been made. All of us admired him
greatly; he was our hero.

One almost unbelievable item: while driving, Ed had
to wear a leather corsetlike affair around his waist to hold
his vital organs firmly in place. This was because the
jouncing of the truck due to the solid rubber tires was so
great that eight hours a day of it had sent him to the
doctor; thus the leather contraption.

Mr. Hodgson drove his Packard car and went on
ahead of the expedition, found camping places, asked to
use them, carried any boys who became sick, as a couple
of them did, and did other errands. He also searched out
the right roads, the road-marking system of 1921 being
completely inadequate in comparison with today's.

The trip was supposed to take two days. Today
almost any truck could handle it in five hours. The
second day out, the expedition ran into a thunder storm
with its resulting downpour. Ed Wild pulled off to the
side of the road, spread a heavy tarpaulin across the top
of the stakes of the stake-body and fastened it down. The
boys huddled under it, keeping fairly dry; but waiting out
the storm took time.

I didn't know any of this, and at the cottage I was
the victim of a crescendo of excitement and waiting. I
looked for the truck all afternoon. I even went up to the
road, sat on the gate, and waited.

About eight-thirty in the evening the Packard arrived with Mr. Hodgson and Mr. Albee and some of the
boys. The weather was good and the newcomers
stretched out on the lawn in their blanket rolls and slept
fitfully, still waiting for the truck.

At about one o'clock Friday morning the truck

arrived. It was too late to pitch tents and these boys, too, unrolled their blankets, rolled up in them again, and stretched out on the ground. The thing I remember was the bright moonlight and the forms lying every-which-way there on the ground.

The next morning after we had eaten breakfast, we pitched the tents and organized the camp. There were two big tepee-type tents, a couple of medium-sized wall tents, and several pup tents.

On the theory that our "woodshed facilities" would not stand up very well under the assault of some thirty visitors, we dug a latrine the other side of the garden next to the fence. This was a deep trench over the top of which we had built a sort of scaffolding designed for rest and rumination. You could sit on it if you were agile.

It worked out adequately, but it had two glaring lacks. It lacked comfort and it lacked privacy. The stoical learned to endure the lack of comfort. But the lack of privacy was with us clear to the end of the expedition. The latrine was hidden from the cottage by the woodshed, and from the rest of the camp area by some wispy and inadequate cornstalks. To the south and to the east, though, only distance shielded you. Your sole consolation was that if there had been any females anywhere in those fields, they would have been as obvious to you as you would have been to them. You only hoped that the farmhouse a quarter of a mile away, which to you seemed to stick up there like a sore thumb, did not harbor a set of field glasses.

One of the boys was so horrified by the openness of the situation that no set of rules, no reprimands, no punishments, kept him from using the red woodshed. The other boys began to call him "Red House," and the name stuck to him for many years afterward.

We did all the things in the two weeks that I had done in the course of eighteen summers. We did the obvious things, like fishing (one night after supper with almost all the boys fishing, we caught enough perch for the whole troop), and swimming, and boating, and ball-playing. We did many of the not-so-obvious things like taking a day to see Fort St. Frederick, Fort Crown Point and Fort Ticonderoga. We climbed Bald Peak. Most of the younger scouts went around through Port Henry to the back side of the mountain by truck, but a few of us crossed the lake by boat and climbed the mountain from the lake side. The truck took many of us to church each Sunday.

One afternoon we all went to Lake View Cemetery where, within sight of the cottage, we held a memorial service for my father, our former scoutmaster.

We did about everything that thirty active minds could think of to do; we pretty thoroughly blanketed that corner of Vermont and Lake Champlain. Everywhere we went everybody smiled and waved and was interested in the big red Queensbury Mills truck with its Worcester-to-Lake Champlain sign. We sang a lot and gave organized cheers—"a big America"—for each place we stopped or for anybody we talked with. People seemed to like that, and they crowded around the truck and asked questions, which we answered. There was no communication gap between them and us; quite the contrary.

Mrs. Hodgson came up on Thursday of the second week and stayed with my mother in the cottage. We crowded around when the Packard brought her and I guess Jack sniffed a couple of times, because the first thing she asked him was, "Jack, have you got a handkerchief?"

Jack said, "Sure. Do you need to borrow it?"

We kidded Jack a good deal about that and he said, "Well how was I to know? She's always borrowing one from me."

At first there were two whole weeks, but the days kept sliding past. Pretty soon there was only one week left, then only three days, then only one. Never had the cottage area known so much activity, so much shouting back and forth, so much singing. Never had the swimming area seen so much splashing. There had never before been so many boats out all at one time so constantly in our particular area. Nor, for that matter, showing such poor oarsmanship.

Then finally came the day of departure. I was to ride back to Worcester on the truck with the others. My mother was to travel by train.

We rose early, took down the tents, packed them aboard the truck. We packed ourselves in, and with one last "big America" for Cliff-top and another for Lake Champlain, we started our homeward trip.

Having come up through Vermont, the truck drove down by way of Lake George, Saratoga and Albany so that the scouts could see different things and different places. We camped at Burnt Hill, in a pasture next to a farmhouse. We lay on the ground under the stars and were wakened by trucks with farm produce driving early to be at the city market when it opened. Since we were all awake we cooked breakfast over an open fire and started on about 8 A.M.

We stopped to visit points of interest, talked to people, watched the scenery of the Berkshires unfold. And finally we reached Worcester at one-thirty in the morning.

So ended the visit of the greatest number of guests at one time that our cottage and its grounds had ever known. We had had guests before, and have had them since; sometimes quite a number at once. But never in numbers even remotely approaching the thirty of that encampment. At last I had reached my goal: practically all my friends had visited the cottage. And all at once, too.

I'd be all for giving a "big America" for Troop 24.

9

What We Did Instead

This matter of entertainment I haven't covered very well. What did we do in the evenings? Whatever did we find to fill the time now taken up by listening to the radio, watching television, going to drive-in movies, or just plain flitting around the roads?

Maybe the reason I've mentioned it only obliquely in passing is because nothing I can say will seem like much in comparison with staggering to bed walleyed after watching two football games in the afternoon and three situation comedies in the evening on TV.

For one thing, how could going to the store or the barbershop in the evening hoping to hear Matt Smith and one of his cronies start a rumor, compete with football and situation comedies?

Well, we thought it was pretty interesting and we wouldn't have missed an occasional rumor-start for the world. The real problem was to be at the right place at the right time and to keep your face very serious.

Matt Smith isn't his right name, but he lived in Addison. At one time, in my days at the cottage, there was a small barbershop in Addison, and Addison boasted two stores. Matt might choose to grace any one of them, and if you got there ahead of him you picked the one that had people around who didn't know Matt very well.

Matt would come in and size up the situation, and if he sat down you knew you were in luck and that a try would be made.

There'd be a silence and then Matt would say, "Too bad about Joe Jones. Is he out of danger yet?"

We'll say the barber was the one he picked to talk to. The barber would not have the foggiest notion what direction the conversation was to take but he wouldn't really have to know. All he'd have to do would be to keep it alive, and add to it each time he spoke. Earnestly. Sympathetically.

"Oh my, no," he'd say. "He had a very bad night last night." Then to give Matt a chance he'd say, "That disease doesn't give you much sleep."

Matt's face would get very long and he'd nod his head.

"Some of those foreign diseases are pretty horrible. Pretty hush-hush, too. They're saying now that he might have caught it from germs carried on a letter from his aunt in Nicaragua."

"I heard that, but I don't know as I believe it." The barber would pause and look puzzled. Actually he'd be trying to think of something to add. "Still, he had to catch it from *some*one or *some*thing. Lack of sleep would be the worst."

Matt's active mind would take it from there.

"Yeah. How can you sleep standing up? They say that if you lie down they won't guarantee that you'll *ever* get up again."

"That's right. The minister stopped in to see him and there he stood in the middle of the floor, his eyes wide open, snoring like all getout. A nurse was holding him up. Gave a person a funny feeling, the minister said."

You get the idea. There'd be more (or less) depending on how the stranger was reacting. I never happened to be near by the next day when the victim of Matt's spoof would come face-to-face with a healthy Joe Jones in Vergennes. But there would be those who did see the encounter and would relay the details with relish.

Mostly these routines did nobody any harm. Once,

though, Matt overstepped. He killed off one of the local citizens in a horrible logging tragedy, and two of the citizen's relatives arrived from Ticonderoga two days later for the funeral. They were met at the door by the deceased. It must have given them a rather nasty start.

Matt was sorry about that. The citizen never spoke to him again.

Starting a rumor, the way Matt did it, was really an art. Your expression, your words, everything had to be exactly right. And as an artist Matt couldn't help performing even when he was the one who'd suffer.

One time he was filling his silo and one of the gang hired to tread down the ensilage inside, looked over the rim at Matt on the ground. When Matt saw him, on the spur of the moment he ran over to a pile of fence rails, grabbed one, ran back and jammed it into the ground, then propped the other end against the bottom of the silo. Then he stood back and anxiously surveyed the silo.

One of the crew yelled over to him, "Does she seem to be holding, Matt?"

And Matt called back, "I think that rail is holding her. She doesn't seem to be listing any more than she was."

The treading gang came right down out of there, refused to believe it was a joke at first; and when they did, were mad. They went home. The whole crew was held up by the happening. Matt was lucky that they were near the top with the ensilage or the hold-up would have been worse.

I've spoken about the Ladies Aid "sociables" at the church. That was another entertainment bit which probably wouldn't have held up very well in comparison with, for instance, today's nude movies.

But the sociables did have their points. For one thing, they were a lot more personal. You might only have been holding hands with a pretty girl under the table at the sociable, but she was there, and alive, and

98

the hand was warm. And you could practically feel the electricity sparking between you. The movie would be just a big shadow on a screen that didn't have much to offer *you*.

Another thing, when you had farm women preparing the refreshments, the eating at a sociable was tops. Just superb. They kept pressing more food on you, and with me they didn't have to press very hard. There were people there that you knew and liked, and to whom you were glad of a chance to talk. It was gay. There were ice-cream sociables, strawberry sociables, and many other kinds.

Also it wasn't just a case of dropping by, the way it is now. In those days we had to plan ahead. We had to figure some way to *get* to an event—any event. Mostly for us it boiled down to three methods: getting a ride on land, going by boat, or walking. Or maybe some combination of the three.

Some of the sociables were held on private lawns, but most of them were held at the West Addison Community House next door to the Methodist Church. You couldn't row anywhere near there, and if you walked it was about four miles each way. Good long miles at that. You had to start in the late afternoon. Going was a major undertaking.

In the late summer and early fall each church in the area would put on a chicken-pie supper. Chicken-pie suppers are still held in Vermont; the state is famous for them. You went to several of these—and probably still do. West Addison had a hickory-nut pie (which I've mentioned) that was like a pecan pie, and was out of this world.

The entertainments at the Community House were something, too. We had transportation for those because they wanted my father and mother to perform, but there were also rehearsals. There were a lot more of the sociables and the entertainments than there are now because your life was held within a narrower radius than it is today. I can't see that it made much difference. There were just so many hours a week that you wanted to spend socializing or getting ready to socialize. We got less variety than is available to country people now. But we were never dissatisfied, because there was no place else to go even if we *had* been dissatisfied, and we hadn't experienced a lot of livelier entertainment to compare it with.

They even held an occasional debate, when those were in style, and those too were interesting. They held one once on the subject "Resolved: That the Negro has contributed more to our civilization than the Indian." They got a French Canadian farmer to be one of the Affirmative team. He got pretty excited and when he got up he said, "That dam' Injun, he go out into the dam' forest and pickie out the biggest dam' tree he can find and he cut he all up into little dam' strinkets and——"

But by then bedlam had broken loose and he couldn't go on. A community house that could boast such a debate couldn't have been *all* dull.

One summer while I was still in high school, and while Sid Gage was visiting me at the cottage, we even played a series of basketball games at the Community House. West Addison played against Addison. Sid and I had no ride, so we walked over there carrying a lunch which we ate on the way over. In it was potato salad that my mother had made for us. When we opened the lunch and Sid saw the potato salad, he had misgivings because he had never been able to digest potato salad adequately.

But it was too late to worry then. It was a case of eat it or eat nothing, and, like all boys that age, he was hungry.

We played the game and it was a rugged experience for Sid and me. We were used to playing on regular-sized basketball courts under strict refereeing that held bodily contact to a minimum.

100

What We Did Instead

The West Addison Community House was no Madison Square Garden. The two foul-lines and the center-jump circle were all mixed up together in the center of the floor, which gives you some idea of how small the playing area was. There was no out-of-bounds on three sides of the playing floor.

The first time I got the ball, two guys jumped on me. I got up hopping mad; no foul had been called. Sid had the same experience. After a few minutes of this we called time-out and Sid and I talked together.

Sid said, "This is the way they play. It isn't going to get any better, and those farm boys are *strong*. Get rid of the ball the instant you get it, before they have a chance to jump you."

After that things went better. We put on a fancy passing exhibition, but believe me it wasn't that we were trying to impress. It was strictly self-preservation. But it did score baskets.

I honestly can't remember who won that first game. I think we did. But what stands out in my mind was the type of play. You put ten boys in a very limited area, and everybody is close to everybody else all the time. Remember, too, that when we started to play we had already walked four miles to get there.

After the game we had to walk home. Sid got quieter and quieter as we walked. Finally when we were within sight of the cottage, he suddenly set down his uniform case on one end, set himself down on its other end, and was very sick indeed.

The potato salad had at last rebelled against all the indignities of the evening and had returned.

Surely this has to be a record of some kind for wanting to play a game of basketball.

There also were dances held around the neighborhood. When I first spent my summers at the cottage I knew nothing about these and cared less. But later on my attitude underwent a 100 percent reversal.

101

There were two kinds of dances: the public dances held in the Addison or Panton halls, and the "kitchen tunks" held in some farmhouse. There were no dances at the West Addison Community House because dancing was not allowed there.

The farmhouse affairs featured mostly square dances, with an occasional "round figure" added. The "hall" dances were every other dance round, and every other dance square. By "square" I don't mean conservative, the way the word is used so much today. "Square" described a dance with four couples facing each other from four sides of a square, and from that basic position going through the turns and "figures" which the "caller" called out to them to execute. These figures were often very intricate and the dances were most impressive when they were done right. And country people could do them right.

Being a city boy I had learned to round-dance, but not to square-dance. This cramped my style somewhat, but not enough to keep me from attending. The transportation problem could usually be solved by walking to the dance, then seeing who had come from farther away than the cottage in that direction. You could then dance with the ladies in that party and, by careful hinting, get yourself an invitation to ride home.

Transportation, as you can see, was inevitably all mixed up with entertainment. In the early years you started to walk some place and hoped someone would come along with a horse and wagon and pick you up. After a few years it began to be a car or a truck that might come along and do the picking-up. This evolved— as the number of cars increased and you grew older— into what later became known as hitchhiking. We used to call it "bumming."

In the area of the cottage the roads were all dirt roads, and the traffic was much too limited to make bumming less than a gamble. The road that passed nearest the cottage might go half a day with no vehicle traveling on it. The idea of waiting beside the road till you got a ride never occurred to anyone: you might have still been there two or three hours later. The technique was never to start for any place farther away than you could hike to if worse came to worst.

To keep it from being too much of a gamble, Sid and I had further techniques. We knew that a friend of ours, Archie Bodette, drove the milk truck to Vergennes every morning from the Chimney Point area. If we got out to a point about two miles from the cottage by eight o'clock, he'd pick us up. Sometimes we'd go to Vergennes just for the ride and a banana split at the drugstore. We'd divide the cost of a banana split for Archie between us. We helped him load and unload milk cans. When he got back to the corner where he'd picked us up, he'd let us out and we'd walk the rest of the way home.

If we wanted to go to Middlebury we'd ride to Vergennes with Archie and then bum to Middlebury on the main road. We wouldn't go from Addison to Middlebury, the short way, because traffic was so skimpy.

Sid's and my bumming efforts finally reached a climax one day when we rowed across the lake to Mullen Brook and bummed up to Westport, New York. I knew a girl who waited on table at Westport Inn, and our hope was that she'd get a friend for Sid and we'd go to a dance. This didn't work out because the girl I knew had a date already, but we got invited to a corn-roast, and it was about midnight when we got out onto the main road and started to walk the five or six miles to Mullen Brook and our boat. The idea of a ride did not occur to us because nobody would pick up anyone bumming at night, even back then.

But, after half a mile or so, lights appeared behind us, and Sid got his thumb ready and made the appropriate gesture with it, not expecting any results.

Much to our surprise the car—it was a touring car—slowed and stopped. We ran to it and there were two men in the front seat.

One of them said, "We've got the back seat full but if you can ride on the load we'll give you a lift."

We piled in—and we had to crawl *up* to do it. We were lying on a load of something lumpy and we were close to the car's top. We didn't dare talk to each other but we were both examining the load by sense of touch. Everything was rough cloth, but under the cloth the lumpy cargo felt to me like bottles.

About then Sid took my hand and guided it to an opening in the cloth. And then I could feel the bottles for sure.

This was during Prohibition, and by now we realized what the cargo was. The rough cloth was burlap. We both knew that bootleggers carried booze bottles in burlap bags in the trunk and back seat of a car. And that the cars had reinforced springs so they'd ride normally even with a full load.

We lay on the bottles; and I don't know about Sid, but I was scared and wished I was anywhere but right there. About then one of the men shifted position a little. And outlined against the beam of the headlights on the road we could see that he had a rifle in his hand, the butt resting on the floor. Sid poked me and I knew he had seen it too.

After that I was *really* scared. I kept wondering what would happen if, when we got to Mullen Brook, they refused to stop or let us out. One thing I knew for sure: I wasn't going to give them any argument.

We rode that way, and I can assure you that lying on a load of bottles isn't the easiest thing in the world on your anatomy. But I can also assure you that this fact was 'way in the background. I hardly thought about the discomfort. I had too much else to think about.

Finally we came to the hill that goes down to the bridge over Mullen Brook.

Sid started to speak and his voice squeaked. And then the words came out several notes higher in pitch than usual:

"We'd like to get out just before this next bridge."

Neither man said anything and the car kept right on. And I thought, "Oh-boy, oh-boy."

Then the brakes went on and relief surged through me. Only a minute or so more. Only a minute or so.

Then the car stopped and we rolled out. We thanked the men profusely and faded into the darkness as the car started on.

Safely out on the lake in our skiff we talked braver and braver. Sid even said he wished he'd had the presence of mind to take a couple of bottles out of that open burlap bag. "They'd never have missed them."

I didn't say anything, but the idea completely horrified me. Visions of the guy putting a flashlight beam on us as we were disembarking while Sid stood there holding a couple of bottles, were very vivid in my mind. On the trip across the lake we lapsed into prolonged periods of silence now and then. I think maybe Sid hadn't felt as much at ease as he would have liked me to believe he had. And as for me, I knew I'd been scared and still was. How I now appeared on the surface had nothing whatever to do with it.

We slept late that morning, but the next morning we rode to Vergennes with Archie and bummed down to Middlebury.

When we started back to Vergennes in the afternoon, two or three cars ignored us where the road goes along the side of Chipman Hill. Then a car slowed down to pick us up. When we came up alongside it, I suddenly realized that it was the same car that had picked us up in New York State two nights before, going the other way.

We opened the back door and got in. And this time there were no burlap bags of bottles. We sat on the seat. But the profiles of the two men, except for the rifle, were exactly the ones we had seen from that back seat two nights before. The men gave no sign that they recognized us. But I think they did. They had had a good look at us in the headlights the other time. That was probably why they had stopped for us *this* time. The reason we hadn't recognized *them* was because all we had seen of the car when they had approached us before had been two headlights.

We got out in Vergennes and thanked them again, maybe trying to change our voices a little so they wouldn't recognize us—in case they hadn't.

When they had gone on, Sid said, "They were heading to Canada for another load. They'll be coming down the other side of the lake tonight. Go empty one way, go full the other, so they won't be noticed as much."

We were both of us a bit subdued. I don't think I ever had a car stop for me for years afterward without thinking about those two men and that tonneau of booze bottles.

One time we rowed up to Westport—we didn't choose to walk at night any more after that—and near midnight, when we were ready to start home, it began to rain. So we turned over the skiff and put our things under it. And then we slept under the slanting roof over a lumber pile designed to keep the boards dry.

It kept *us* dry too. It was about a foot and a half high at one end, sloping down to the top of the lumber pile at the other end. It was not the softest bed I ever had, but up there on top of the lumber, with a couple of blankets to keep us warm, we got a pretty good night's sleep.

And then there was the time we took the canoe-skiff the length of Lake George. That was after Labor Day, and again it was Sid Gage who was with me.

106

You have only a very few completely idyllic periods in your lifetime, and this was one in mine.

One of us rowed and the other paddled, and we swapped places every fifteen minutes. We traveled on Lake Champlain until we had nearly reached the town of Ticonderoga, and then we started up the river that links Champlain with Lake George.

We began to see signs on the trees along the bank advertising portage services for small boats. Trucks would take you and your boat past the falls and deposit you on the other side of Ticonderoga at the beginning of Lake George. We hired one of the trucks.

We re-embarked late in the afternoon, and that night we burrowed into a haystack and slept in a field beside Lake George. Haystacks have been made obsolete by the field-bailer, but in those days of loose hay, every field used to have one or more.

It rained the next afternoon and we took refuge in the icehouse of a boys' camp, closed for the season and deserted. We slept on the sawdust in the icehouse, which would be used again the next winter to cover the ice when it was harvested in chunks from the frozen lake.

From that time on we stayed entirely on islands. These were owned by the state, each had at least one permanent tent floor, and in the summer they were assigned to those who made application for them at an office housed near the Narrows. We didn't have to do this.

We wouldn't have found any island campsites available before Labor Day, but after the season was over, everything was deserted. We'd stop in the late afternoon, find a tent floor that, due to the slope of the land, had room underneath it. We'd turn the canoe-skiff over with one end on the tent floor, and we'd sleep partly under the canoe and partly under the tent floor. After we'd made camp, we'd have a swim. On most islands you could dive into the water right from the rocks. The water was crystal clear, as it always was at that time in Lake George.

We'd build a fire and cook our dinner. We'd clean our dishes and then fix up a backrest facing the fire. We'd sit there with the night noises around us—a splashing fish, a heron's squawk, a dog barking on the mainland. The dusk would gradually turn to dark.

Every night we'd tell each other the plots of movies which one of us had seen and the other hadn't. By nine o'clock we'd be in bed.

In the morning we'd swim again before we dressed. Then we'd cook and eat breakfast, pack, and start on.

The wind blew all that time from the south, against us. It was slow, hard going. From one particularly satisfying camp at the Narrows we went on to Lake George village, at the far end of the lake, arriving there by midafternoon. After walking around the town awhile, we went back to the skiff, tied a blanket between two oars, held that up in fifteen-minute shifts for a sail, and let the south wind carry us back to the Narrows for another night at the campsite we had occupied the previous night.

The next day the wind was still south, so we tied the blanket between the oars again and whooshed over the remainder of the 40-mile-long lake in one day. In fact we went so fast that we had a close call in passing Tongue Mountain. A gust of wind, swirling around the mountain, took one gunwale under the water before we could drop the blanket.

With water swashing in the bottom, we rowed ashore and emptied the boat; then we wrung out various articles, and saved what food we could. We rowed the rest of the way to Ticonderoga and were carried through town by truck. We made camp that night opposite Fort Ticonderoga on Lake Champlain. The fort's parapets and guns were right above us. The campsite we chose couldn't have been too far from the spot from which

Ethan Allen's men embarked to capture it nearly a century and a half before.

We hadn't been bothered by mosquitoes throughout the trip. But that night we had them. Boy, did we have them. We tried everything, even to covering ourselves completely with a blanket and using the cardboard center from a toilet-paper roll as a chimney to breathe through. Mosquitoes came down our chimney and bit us on the nose.

About eleven o'clock we gave up, packed our duffel, put up the blanket between the two oars, and started on.

The wind was strong. The night was cloudy, but you could see well enough to navigate. The lights on shore slid by. A train, brightly lighted, slithered past on the New York shore. Every fifteen minutes we changed places.

It was a completely lovely night. We passed under the Champlain Bridge and landed about three in the morning on the shore down below the Hoyt farm. This was a couple or three miles nearer than the cottage was.

We were in no mood to travel the extra miles to get home, so we turned the boat over and put our duffel under it. Then we walked the three-quarters of a mile up to the farm buildings. We went into the hay barn and spread our blankets in the mow, and we had no trouble falling asleep.

Just as we were going to sleep we heard it start to rain. It was still raining in the morning. It rained for three solid days.

The farmer who ran the farm was named George. When George came out to milk in the morning and stepped into the barn, we rose up and said, "Good morning, George." It's a wonder he didn't have a heart attack.

So even if we had no entertainment to compete with football on TV and situation comedies, we did have our moments of enjoyment and excitement. And certainly we got exercise enough to keep us healthy.

I'm not sure I'd have swapped TV in front of an armchair for the things we did in its place.

10

Winter on Lake Champlain

During the early years of my life I saw the cottage and Lake Champlain only during July and August.

My mother and my father used to tell people, "We spend our summers on Lake Champlain and our winters in Worcester." As a child I took this to mean 50–50. This misconception accentuated the speed with which the time at the cottage flashed past and the time in Worcester dragged along. School probably had a great deal to do with this, only I didn't realize it.

I didn't see the lake in winter until I was in college at Middlebury, some eighteen miles from the lake. When I did see it I could hardly believe what I saw. Champlain in winter and Champlain in summer are two completely different worlds.

The world of winter on Lake Champlain is just as beautiful as the summer world, but in an entirely different way. It's a white world trimmed with black. The vast expanse of snow-covered ice is blindingly white in bright sunlight, and beyond the lake the snow-covered mountains have splotches and lines of black, which are the dark evergreens. The deciduous trees, without their leaves, show at that distance as gray or a spider-webby black, depending on how thick the grove is. There are infinite variations to this, depending on the depth of snow, the time of year, the light. Always, though, even in the brightest sunshine, the scene looks incredibly cold.

Right out on the ice of the lake there are clusters of small buildings, the famous fish shanties from which devotees fish through the ice for smelt and perch, and which are moved out on runners as soon as the ice is thick enough to hold them. They are left there all winter. From in front of the cottage I have counted as many as two hundred of these fish shanties in several large concentrations, plus scattered singles.

If there is no snow, the ice of the lake looks black. Figures skim across it on skates to and from the shanties, and cars streak across its surface. You might even see the sail of an iceboat if there was no snow.

Usually there is snow. Seldom is it very deep; the wind, with its long uninterrupted sweep, takes care of that. Only a heavy snowfall without wind builds depth on the lake's surface. To hold that depth it needs to be a wet snow that will crust over. Otherwise the first strong wind after the storm will turn the lake into a huge basin of swirling snow, much of it traveling till it hits the shore.

In my father's day you saw men skating or walking to their shanties, and horse-drawn sledges moving from one concentration of the little buildings to another. Later you saw cars moving over the ice if the snow wasn't too deep. And in recent years there have been the snowmobiles. In between, there appeared a hybrid affair called a snow-buggy made from an old car, featuring huge tires, usually equipped with chains, and a homemade body. These are unregistered, parked on shore, and used only on the lake.

I wish I had one cent for every pound of smelt or perch that has been harvested through those Lake Champlain fish shanties over the generations. King Midas, move over for a guy with a really ambitious idea!

In my own family, I know that my grandfather

fished smelt from a shanty. My father did, I have, my daughter has; and my grandchildren may have already—if not, they soon will. I think maybe it goes further back than that, but I don't *know.*

The style in shanties has changed very little over the years. The materials and the size have changed some, that's about all. They are very light in construction, and are mounted on a set of runners that are usually removed once the shanty has been dragged to location. If you don't remove the runners you'd better anchor the shanty with a rope tied to the middle of a piece of broomstick or some such. You push the broomstick lengthwise through one of the holes in the ice and then pull it up sideways against the hole underneath the ice, and fasten the rope to the main frame of the shanty. It's not a bad idea to anchor the shanty anyway, because the windward wall, on that flat expanse of lake, acts like a sail. The shanty of a friend of mine started off across the glare ice once in a high wind.

When it passed the shanty of a friend of *his* he yelled, "Rob, Rob, where am I going?"

And Rob called back, "Depends on the life you've led, Charlie."

The door of the shanty is in the middle of the long side. Opposite the door is the stove. The stoves used to burn wood or coal, now they mostly burn oil. There are two seats set against the two short sides of the shanty. These face each other. Between them are four square holes in the floor set over four holes in the ice. Each man fishes the two holes nearest him, a line in each hand.

The lines are wound on specially made fish-sticks about a foot and a half long. Some men who fish a lot become very adroit at handling these sticks when a smelt bites. You hold the sticks, one in each hand with the long end pointing away from you, and you catch the line first with one stick then the other until the fish comes through the hole. A quick snap lands him in your pail if he is not hooked well. (If he's hooked solidly you'll have to waste

time taking him off the hook.) Then, after a quick look at the bait, you point both sticks at the hole and let the line slide off them. The heavy sinker straightens out the line and carries the bait down again to the fish. You have lost very little time.

Most of us aren't that adroit. For us there is a hook, or maybe just a nail, in each side wall of the shanty. When you hook a fish on your lefthand line, you flip your righthand line over this hook and have both hands free to pull in your fish. When your righthand line catches the fish you flip your lefthand line over *its* hook.

When you pull in a fish using both hands that way, the wet line usually lands in your lap. Sometimes you are fishing down sixty or a hundred feet, or even more. This means a lot of wet line in your lap a lot of times. So I, for one, wear the rubber pants of a rain suit when I'm shanty-fishing.

Obviously the bait will have to be changed every little while. Usually you try to do this during a lull in the biting. For bait you use a very thin slice of smelt, about an inch and a half long and one-fourth to three-eighths of an inch wide, cut from the side of a smelt you have already caught. You hook it by one end and let it dangle. That's all; just that silver strip.

But when the sinker gets down to the fishing area and stops, the unweighted snell and hook, which have been following, float out and down more slowly. If you pull your line up and down—this is called "jigging"—it makes your bait dart in and up, then out and down, making it look like a tiny frenetic silver minnow. So you jig rapidly several times, then hold your line still for a moment or so to make it easy for the smelt to bite, then jig again. You do this over and over.

There are refinements. Some fishermen use a "flasher," a long silver sinker, which, during the jigging process, is supposed to look like a silver fish chasing the small silver minnow. This is supposed to excite the smelt, make them want to be in on the kill.

As I say, sometimes you fish in more than a hundred feet of water. At such times it is very hard to tell whether or not you have a fish on. The average smelt is about six to eight inches long and not very heavy. They grow a lot bigger than that, but they also grow smaller.

Sometimes, though, you will find that the fish bite best within twelve or fifteen feet of the ice. This is particularly true toward the spring of the year. At such times you can cover the windows of the shanty on the inside, for a darkened interior lets you see farther, and more clearly, into the water. From there you can watch your bait perform and see the fish bite. And when you do this you'll be completely astonished.

We'll say that you have been fishing for the last fifteen minutes without a single bite. You are convinced there are no smelt down there. You look down, and to your vast amazement there are dozens of smelt swimming slowly back and forth close to your bait, paying absolutely no attention to it.

Then, for no apparent reason, one of them will suddenly dash in and grab that bait, and you'll have another fish. If you hadn't seen with your own eyes what happened you would think one stray just happened along.

Or, more amazing even than that, one of the slow swimmers may suddenly charge in and bunt the flasher or sinker. This feels exactly like a bite on the hook, and if your line was deep you'd think you missed your chance.

It's no easy blow they give the sinker, either: it's a good solid clout. And afterward they sort of stagger away dazed, if a small fish can be said to stagger. They make it obvious, anyway, that they are pretty shocked and disillusioned by the whole turn of events. They move away on a wavy course like a drunk on a sidewalk. I have

115

always figured that they think they are attacking a relatively soft interloper, but who knows?

When you are talking about a good catch of smelt you are not talking about single fish, you are talking about pounds of fish. You hear fishermen say, "I got about fifteen pounds of smelt." Or twenty, or twenty-five. And it takes a tremendous number of slim, six-inch fish to make a pound. You can sell your surplus (dressed) to the markets and stores or to people who have left a standing order with you; or you can give them to friends (before dressing them) and get out of a fast but messy job. When you go home you leave several smelt in the shanty as bait "to get started on" the next time you fish.

Fishermen are somewhat reticent about letting you know what they have caught. They're afraid you'll cut them off, or try to, by moving your shanty between them and the direction from which the smelt seem to be moving. This is no idle fear, either. I've been having good luck and been cut off so completely that after it happened I didn't get half a dozen more fish.

On this matter of reticence, once I stopped at the shanty of a friend of mine. He and his companion had half a pail of fish when I opened the door and looked in on them. But when they saw who it was, they produced a big pack-basket full from under one seat. The small catch in the bucket had been window-dressing for strangers.

There is quite a bit of shanty-moving. You find out about a place where big catches are being made, and you go there. It is productive for a day or a week, and then it peters out; and you hear of another spot.

Besides the smelt, you catch a few blue runners and quite a few perch. Sometimes when you are fishing in shallow areas you catch more perch than smelt. Ordinarily, though, this is not the case.

And then once in a great while there comes the nerve-jarring excitement of feeling something *big*. It could be a big northern pike (I've seen a shanty-caught pike that was over three feet long—and what a battle he must have put up), or a ling or a carp; something like that. Once I talked to a man who had caught a six-pound lake trout when he was fishing for smelt.

Such a catch presents tremendous problems and you're lucky if you pull it off. To begin with, the average smelt-hole just wouldn't be big enough to let a fish like that through. And the average smelt line wouldn't stand the strain of lifting him out even if the hole was big enough. And with two-foot-thick ice you'd have your work cut out for you to maneuver the fish's head up into the bottom of the hole so you could reach a hand down to his gills.

Or if the hole should prove to be too small, you would have a fantastic time enlarging it with a sharp chisel while your companion tried to keep a tight line on the fish and at the same time keep that line out of the way so that you wouldn't inadvertently cut it while you were trying to chop the ice.

The only good thing about such a contest is that if you *do* bring it off, you'll never forget any heart-rending detail of the fight as long as you live.

All this and comfort too. You sit there in shirt-sleeves, comfortable and warm while the wind howls outside. Maybe it's a zero day; you don't care, except that you've got to make the trip back to shore if you have walked or skated out.

At noon you let down the hinged table attached to the inside of the door. You eat, and usually you keep on fishing while you do so. Nobody ever seems to get enough smelt-fishing. Usually the smelt slow their biting around noon or early afternoon, but they start biting again around three or four o'clock. Some smelt fishermen put a bright lantern on the ice just outside the shanty and fish at night with fairly good luck. The light seems to call the smelt.

In the late spring, just before the ice goes out, the

smelt tend to congregate next to shore near the edge of open water. Your shanties are off the lake by then, and you fish out in the open. The smelt you catch are very small, and are called "snapfish." They usually grab the bait, catch their teeth in it. The pull you give has to be slower and steadier than for hooked smelt. The moment you give them slack they can, and do, let go. There's a technique to catching snapfish. It all boils down to not pulling hard enough to rip the fish's teeth out of the bait, yet pulling very steadily.

Who fishes in these shanties? People from all walks of life—men, women, children. Mostly they are people who live within driving distance of Champlain. But weekends they come from hundreds of miles away to rent a shanty for the day, and fish.

The regulars, the people who fish nearly every day, fall mostly into two categories: retired people and farmers. Retired people are likely to be a bit old for downhill skiing, and a winter of watching television morning, noon and night doesn't thrill them much. And dairy farmers in winter, once the morning chores are out of the way, can find a lot of time before evening chores if they really like fishing.

Modern transportation and road-plowing have tremendously widened the radius that people can travel to fish smelt in Champlain.

In my grandfather's day, and in my father's, the shanties were wider, at least six feet on the short side. This was to allow for a couple of hinged bunks above the two fishing seats; these could be folded up out of the way in the daytime and slept in at night. Nearby farmers would drive a horse and sleigh to the lake, hire stable space from a lakeside farmer, and live for a week or more in the shanty, fishing. A sledge was sent around each day by an enterprising storekeeper in Port Henry, New York, and the driver took orders for food and supplies, which he delivered on his trip the next day. He also bought the smelt the fishermen had caught, paying twenty-five cents a pound. At the end of his stay the fisherman usually had a pocketful of money. It was like being paid for having a good time, a setup that much appealed to the thrifty Vermont countryman.

My father told about waking early, unhooking the lines and letting them down into the holes, and catching smelt while he lay in bed.

A coal fire would keep the shanty cozy overnight, and provide a surface for cooking the morning's bacon and eggs and toast. Refrigeration was definitely no problem. Neither was water.

In those days when the fish bit very well, the fishermen would substitute a piece of flannel for the strip of smelt as bait. You didn't have to renew the flannel, and a snapfish's teeth would catch in it very nicely.

Lake Champlain freezes in sections. On the average, the area below the Narrows, where the Champlain Bridge is located, and the shallow bays freeze in December. The area between the Narrows and the end of Split Rock Mountain freezes in January. And the broad lake freezes in February. Sometimes during a mild winter the broad lake never freezes clear over. I myself have known two years when even the middle section, above the bridge, all winter froze no farther north than our cottage at Potash Bay.

When the ice first forms below the Narrows, fishermen cut a dozen or more holes and fish pike with tip-ups and minnows. A tip-up has a trigger mechanism and a little red flag. When a fish bites, the flag snaps up and the operator runs or skates over to try to land his fish.

As the season progresses and the ice gets very thick, you either have to give this sport up or engage in it every day. If you don't open the holes every day, digging out a dozen or more holes requires the stamina and physique of a pro halfback in top condition. Even if your muscles and your heart would stand it, you'd be digging during far too much of your fishing time.

The same sort of fishing takes place in the shallow places like Kellogg's Bay. Men fish those bays when the lake outside them is still open. This has definite elements of danger.

A man named Blow, from whom I used to buy fish, was fishing Kellogg's Bay many years ago. The large chunk of ice on which he was operating broke off and began to drift very slowly out into the broad lake with an offshore wind. If he had leaped off when he first discovered what had happened and taken the few strokes to the solid ice of the bay, he might have been saved. But to avoid the icy bath he stuck with the floe. By the time boats had been found and dragged across the ice and a helicopter from Burlington had been sent down, the floe had broken up, and not even Blow's body was ever found.

The combination of Lake Champlain and winter should never be taken lightly. When the ice is solid and the weather is fine, risk is almost non-existent. Still, there are spots even then where currents have undermined the ice near the mouth of a river or brook, making it paper thin—even though the surface looks just like the thick ice near by.

There are cracks and heaves, too. Mostly these are obvious and can be avoided. A heave is *very* obvious. Water expands slightly when it freezes. In small bodies of water this expansion has little noticeable effect. But on Lake Champlain this pressure builds up, finds a weak spot, breaks the surface, and forces the ice up in a long ragged line to ease that expansion pressure. Huge cakes of ice break off at the line and lie at crazy angles, impossible to cross with a car or snowmobile or snow-buggy. An automobile might have to go out of its way for many miles to find a safe place where it could cross.

Very occasionally when the weak spot gives way, it heaves *down* instead of up. These places are really dangerous because the water comes through the break

120

and seeks the level of the main body of ice. If the weather is cold, this water skims over with ice at once and the surface of the lake looks undisturbed. But if you should try to drive, walk, or skate across this spot before the new ice became thick enough to hold you or your car, you'd have a most unexpected and unwelcome bath.

Once I was skating back to the cottage from the Basin Harbor area and I saw a place ahead that looked corrugated, like tiny waves on water. For a split second I wondered how water could freeze this way. And then the horrible truth burst in upon me that it *was* water.

I slewed sideways and stopped at the very edge of open water, the blades of my skates actually wet. I stood there thanking my lucky stars that I had recognized those corrugations in time. It was a reverse heave, and the afternoon temperature was above freezing. I had skated across to the New York shore and north along Split Rock Mountain, so I had had no warning that there would be such a heave on the Vermont side. I had to skate far toward the New York shore again before I found a place to cross.

In addition to the danger of thin ice, there is another hazard which has taken a considerable toll over the years. This is the danger of losing your way on the lake in a swirling snowstorm or blizzard. Remember, the lake is fourteen miles wide at its widest point.

That doesn't sound like much? Believe me, it is. The danger is very real. In the snow, tracks drift level in minutes under really bad conditions, so there is no clue to the right direction. And you can see nothing but swirling snow. Men have wandered or driven in a circle in such a situation, run out of gas or driven a team till the horses dropped, and been found frozen to death.

In my father's boyhood when he lived on the farm near the lake, there was no way to travel to the New York side of the lake except on "winter roads." There was no bridge yet, the ferry of course could not run. You had to go a long way around on land, or cross on the ice. So they crossed on the ice. All sorts of commerce traveled across the lake's frozen surface. Hay, lumber, and coal were carried back and forth in quantity.

And the ingenious New York and Vermont teamsters had a very simple method for solving the losing-your-way problem and keeping their teams on course in the middle of a blizzard. They cut evergreens, mostly cedars, and set them up every few feet beside the winter road. They cut holes in the ice and froze these small trees upright in the holes so they wouldn't blow away.

You followed the line of evergreens and you came to the other side. The evergreens were tall enough so they furnished guidance through even the worst blizzard. They were even plain enough to be followed by a slightly tipsy man who had driven his horse and sleigh over to one of the Port Henry saloons for a night out. If he was too drunk to drive, the horse would probably follow the evergreens for him. And if he had remembered to leave his barn door open he might wake up the next morning in the cutter where it stood on his own barn floor, the horse contentedly munching hay from the mow beside him.

Another winter use for evergreens was to mark the outside edge of an "ice-cutting." When I first came to Lake Champlain the only source of summer ice was the icehouses that were filled with lake ice during the winter. The ice was covered with a thick layer of sawdust, and all summer these ice cakes were used in refrigerators and milk-coolers.

At the cottage every three or four days we used to have to wash the sawdust off a big cake of ice, and with ice tongs lift it into the top ice compartment of our refrigerator. The ice compartment was at the top of the refrigerator because cold air drops, and thus circulated down into the food compartment. From the ice compartment a pipe led down to a point underneath the refrigerator to carry away the water from the melting ice.

You put a pan underneath that pipe, and if human frailty caused you to forget to empty that pan both night and morning, inexorably it would overflow. Boy, would it overflow. All over everything. Unless you were an extremely good talker you would shortly find yourself with a mop, cleaning up the mess.

Most icehouse owners, and they came from many miles each side of the lake to get ice, did not have the equipment or the tools to cut and harvest ice. So some enterprising man who did, would start an ice-cutting. He would sell ice to each person who came with a sledge for it, at so much per cake, loaded onto the buyer's sledge. He would have the necessary saws, pike poles, loading gear, and help. And he would make out fairly well financially.

In zero weather the open water left by the removal of the day's harvest would freeze over rapidly. If an unwary person came along and tried to walk or drive on it after the men went home, he'd get a monumental surprise. So the operator marked with cut evergreens the boundaries of the harvested area.

The man who was filling his icehouse would place the ice in it cake by cake, in a set pattern. When he had finished putting in the first layer he would start a second right where he had started the first. He would continue with a third, a fourth, and as many more as were required to fill the icehouse. He would pack sawdust in the space between the boards of the building and each layer as he finished it, and would spread a thick layer of sawdust on top when he had finished placing the last layer.

When he took the ice out the next summer he would remove the last cake first, the next-to-the-last second, just reversing the pattern he had used in putting it in. The scoop shovel you used to move the sawdust you always laid in the hole from which today's cake had been taken. That told you where to dig for tomorrow's cake to maintain the removal pattern.

Nothing would make an icehouse owner swear harder or longer than to have "some bumbling lunkhead" dig a cake out from between two other cakes without regard for his pattern.

Farmers whose barns were close to the shore regularly drove their cows to the lake to drink.

In these days when a drinking cup, automatically refilled by a cow's efforts to get more water, is close to the head of each cow in a stanchion, it is hard to realize that cows were ever driven outdoors to drink; but they were. The drinking rectangles had to be re-opened with a sharp chisel before the cows were let out of the barn, and this required a monumental amount of work. The cows were thirsty and knew where the water was. They might even run to get there. Inevitably sometime—what with all the pushing and shoving for position—a valuable cow would get half into, or maybe even all the way into, the water. It would then take a tripod, a block-and-tackle, and help from the neighbors to get her out.

In such a drinking area, evergreens again were stuck in the ice to warn off the unwary.

The first time you go out on the ice of Lake Champlain on a very cold day, you're likely to be scared half to death by a riflelike sound. It is as if the ice had cracked. It is as if a tremendous crack had opened up right under your feet.

You leap involuntarily; you look around you on all sides with apprehension. You see cracks, but none of them are *that* big. You bravely smother the impulse to run for shore. You are just drawing a relieved breath when the sharp crack comes again, louder, followed by a deep boom. You leap again. It's the beginning of a period of extreme skittishness on your part.

Actually, you have nothing to fear. The ice is "making"—a frightening phenomenon full of sound and fury. It happens when more freezing is occurring, not when ice is melting. Sometimes the cracking and boom-

124

ing are at a distance, muffled. Sometimes they seem to be right under your feet. When a sound like that comes, even the person who knows there's no danger is likely to act about as skittish as a complete neophyte.

Particularly this is true when you are riding in a car out on the ice. A sharp boom from underneath you can be unnerving, to say the least. Really, though, in a car there is always some danger, because a car is a very heavy vehicle. If you avoid all areas of known sharp currents you cut the danger 'way down. But it is always there, at least in your mind. Many times I have ridden out to a fish shanty with the front door of the car ajar and one foot hanging outside. You understand that I knew perfectly well this wasn't necessary. But I just felt I wanted more ventilation. The idea that I was chicken is absurd.

The danger really multiplies in the spring. The ice then is still solid, and winter has the lake still firmly in its grip. But the sun has become very strong and the spring runoff has started. The runoff always raises the level of the lake, causing the ice-sheet to float clear of the shore. There gradually gets to be some ten or fifteen feet of water or thin ice between the solid ice and the solid ground.

This sun, shining with authority now, does unexpected things. One afternoon I went to a shanty that had been in place all winter. It had sheet-metal siding, and the door faced south. It was a sunny day, but the north wind was biting. I reached for the doorlatch and my left leg broke through the ice clear to my hip.

It took several seconds for Lake Champlain's frigid water to work through my heavy clothing, and meanwhile I was grabbing at the threshold as I fell forward. I got my weight onto my arms and my spraddled-out right leg. I tried to get my left leg out of there.

The men in the shanty heard the noise and opened the door. One of them grabbed me by the shoulders and pulled me into the shanty. I was all right except for that one wet leg, and we second-guessed that the spot where I went through had been sheltered from the cold wind and had received a double dose of warm sunlight. It had got the direct sun, plus the sun reflected off that metal siding. This had been going on for days, even weeks. The men who had been fishing in the shanty were most grateful: if I hadn't stopped by to see them, one of them would have been the one to have an icy leg when he quit fishing for the day and stepped outside.

You don't get much skating on Lake Champlain. But when you do get skating it's so different from rink-skating that it's almost unbelievable.

Mostly you get skating early, before the snow cover has arrived. But you may get it again sometime in January, with the January thaw. If the thaw is extensive enough and long enough, the snow melts and the ice-sheet is covered with slush and water. Then when the zero weather comes back, that water freezes and gives you—until the next snowstorm—a skatable surface.

It seems astonishing to a rink-skater to start off in one direction and continue in that direction indefinitely. But this isn't the biggest difference. The biggest difference is in the effect the wind has on you.

When you skate into even a light wind a huge, invisible hand seems to hold you back. You have to stop often to rest. Your legs ache. You don't make much progress. Your strokes are short.

But when you skate *with* even a light wind your strokes lengthen and your speed increases unbelievably. You seem to fly along.

Once I skated from our cottage to the Champlain Bridge against a south wind, and made agonizingly slow, labored progress. My setter dog, Patches, was running with me, taking side excursions, turning and looking back to see if I was coming, cutting circles around me when I stopped to rest. In every way open to him he

126

expressed his contempt for my lack of speed. Come on, Boss, let's make some time!

I turned around at the bridge and started back. And everything was much different. My strokes were long, I swooped over the ice. Patches tried to keep up with me. And now he wasn't making any side trips either.

He began to lose ground (or ice) a little, and then he buckled down to running in real earnest. He gave it everything he had.

Gradually, though, and in spite of his very best efforts, he fell behind. Grudgingly, ever so slowly, he fell farther behind until, when I reached the cottage, he was about sixty yards in back of me. When I stopped and he came up to me he dropped down on the ice and I thought I detected a reproachful look. Never had I moved that fast before to his knowledge, and he disapproved of the whole demeaning experience.

Your skates have to be extra sharp to handle ice that smooth. To anybody used to skating where hundreds of others have skated, the smoothness of the lake's surface is a revelation.

On a pleasant Sunday afternoon when the ice is right you can skate twenty, thirty, even forty miles. You can go by way of Westport on the New York side, up along Split Rock Mountain, and back to the cottage by the Vermont shore. One of the times I made this trip, I found fishermen in the open catching huge ling off Barber's Point—the only time I ever saw these fish caught through the ice.

On the way home we came to one of those heaves I spoke of, and as we approached we could see a black spot against the heaved-up ice. When we drew closer the dark spot got up and stretched, and we realized that it was a fox. He had been lying there in the lee of the ice cakes, a mile or more from shore, spending the day in complete safety, able to see at a great distance any danger that approached.

After he had stretched he began to trot south ahead of us, taking it easy, keeping the same distance between us and him at all times. We weren't skating very fast against a light breeze, and all he had to do was trot.

But we were approaching the cluster of fish shanties over the deep water just south of Potash Point, out from Loomis's dock. All of a sudden he got the human smell on the wind from those shanties. He stopped instantly and stood there sniffing the breeze. He was squarely between them and us.

Then he started off again, this time at a right angle to the direction he had been taking. Now he was headed directly toward the New York shore. He had no intention of being squeezed between two sets of humans. Nor did he have any intention of going to the nearer Vermont shore where something might be lying in wait for him. He didn't move very fast, but he was no longer just loping along.

Instantly the young man who was skating with me started across what amounted to the hypotenuse of a right triangle to intersect his new course. He skated fast.

When the fox saw what was happening we found out what *he* could do in the way of speed. He advanced the gas lever several notches, and all of a sudden he was flying. My friend didn't come even close to cutting him off. Low to the ice and extremely graceful, he became a reddish streak. About all my friend could do was fall in behind him.

From that time on, the space between my friend and the fox widened rapidly in spite of expert speed skating. It widened, that is, until it became about the distance the fox had kept between himself and us earlier; then it stayed there. My friend's wind wouldn't stand a continuous (and fruitless) chase, and he very soon gave up and rejoined me. The last we saw of the fox was a tiny dark speck continuing on toward the New York shore.

There is one more facet to winter on Lake Champlain that people don't understand about. This is the awesome power of the ice when it finally breaks up.

People who have had experience with only small bodies of water don't understand or expect any such frightening power. In a small lake or pond the ice just melts and disappears; there's no power to it. But in Lake Champlain the ice usually breaks up during a hard wind and, driven by that wind, the only word to describe the force it generates is *inexorable.*

Usually the ice does not break up below Split Rock, in the narrower parts of the lake, until the snows on the fields are melted and a big percentage of the mountain snows have come down the streams in the form of water and emptied into the lake.

Before it breaks up, the warm spring sun rots it. The fish shanties have long since been removed. Now only the crows dare walk on its surface and scavenge the used baits and other items left in the areas the shanties occupied. That wide band of open water which I mentioned between the solid ice and the shore is very pronounced now. And a high runoff from the streams continues to raise the level of the lake daily. Signs of spring are everywhere.

On a warm, sunny, still spring day you can look down on the sheet of ice from the cliff at the cottage, and the surface will seem honeycombed. Harder bits of snow or ice will resist the sun longer and will stand up in a feathery design. When they do melt they fall with a tinkling sound. A very warm sun will build this sound until the warm quiet of a spring afternoon is full of its music.

This is called "whispering ice," and once you hear it you will understand why. The sound is not loud; rather, it is muted, subdued. But it is a joyful sound, full of promise.

And then comes the heavy wind. The ice breaks up into large, medium, and small pieces. The wind drives these against the shore. There is nothing spectacular about it; it is almost disappointingly docile. The ice field moves only inches at a time. There is no crashing, no driving of cakes high on the shore: just an inexorably slow movement forward. But in that movement is vast power. There are thousands of tons of ice behind the first cakes that touch the shore. A dock, a tree, a shanty left too low on the beach, all feel this force. The wind drives against those tons of ice behind the leading edge, and the shore and the dock and the tree remain stationary. Something has to give.

Ice grinds there under this terrible pressure, and the first of it is pushed high on the beach, perhaps even to the trees, if there are trees and the wind is strong enough. But the pressure remains, and weaker cakes give in to it, pop up and are slid in on top of the ice already there. The first layer grinds against the tree trunks. I have seen a big tree trunk chewed more than half through by grinding ice.

This pushing of ice high atop ice already pushed up on shore, goes on a few inches at a time. Boats, if any have been left in harm's way, are crushed like shells. Pilings are pushed over, railway-trestle abutments are destroyed. Nothing can stand against that force, that power.

People who have lived beside the lake understand this, and make sure nothing is left on exposed shores. But strangers, even engineers, often underestimate the power of the ice when it breaks up. Many years ago the Delaware & Hudson Railroad built a trestle across the wide mouth of Bulwagga Bay to take their trains into Port Henry, New York. When the plans were made public, local people pointed out to the engineers that the wind at this particular spot got a twelve- to fifteen-mile sweep, and that the trestle abutments would not stand against the ice.

This seemed absurd to the engineers: ice was a crushable item; they went ahead and built the trestle.

Winter on Lake Champlain

The first time the ice went out, pushed by a hard north wind, it took the whole trestle. Today the Delaware & Hudson comes up into Port Henry on the west side of Bulwagga, not across its mouth. The line of fill and other signs of the engineers' attempt still remain, a silent monument to the power of moving ice.

Because of ice-power there are no boathouses close to the water in any exposed place on Lake Champlain. Docks that are exposed are generally built so they will be underneath the high waters of spring and thus be out of danger. To make doubly certain, most of their tops are built with a flat center but sloping sides, to allow the ice to ride up and over them if the water should be unusually low some spring. Never give the ice a solid crack at a dock.

There are boathouses and docks in sheltered bays, there are boathouses high up on shore with marine railways going into the water; things like that. But mostly the Lake Champlain landowner has a very deep respect for the force of the ice. Even the Burlington Harbor breakwater has sloping sides.

After the ice breaks up with all that power, the lake is, the very next day, surprisingly free of ice. You would expect that for upwards of a week afterward there would be ice floating around. This is not the case. One day it is there in quantity, the next it is gone or almost gone. It's like magic. I've heard the theory advanced that it sinks. This is against all natural laws, but I can well sympathize with the puzzlement that led to the acceptance of such a theory.

And with the disappearance of the ice there is the promise of a new season of boats and canoes and lake commerce; even swimming (though the thought of that makes you shiver at the moment).

In a very short time the cold whiteness, the cars out on the ice, the fish shanties, are only a fading memory, a dream. But not a bad dream. Not at all. Just a very different dream of a very different world.

11

Cliff-top and College

Some people have been unkind enough to intimate that college unrest comes mostly at times when there is nothing interesting going on, or when an exam period is imminent.

Unfortunately, when I was in college there was a modicum of truth in this charge. The great goldfish-swallowing contests and the famous telephone-booth-stuffing efforts in collegiate circles both came in the spring after the basketball season had ended and the baseball, track, tennis and romance seasons hadn't begun. Of course you might say the romance season was always with us, but in spring it really came into its own.

It wasn't that we (and others) didn't have a concern for social problems. We didn't have the news of these problems that blares at us many hours a day nowadays via television. The world was a much smaller place for each of us, somehow. We were too far removed from Africa, for instance, to have much information about it or "concern" in regard to it. Our churches sent missionaries to work among the "heathen" and that was about it on a world-wide basis.

But locally: that was something else. If somebody had bad luck—a fire, a disaster—the neighbors pitched in. It was a vast concern, but very local in nature.

I can still remember a football team captain, out of condition by Christmas, plowing his way through the deep snow in a Santa Claus suit complete with pillow, a heavy pack of presents over his shoulder, Ho-ho-ing across the field in back of the fraternity house to the ecstatic delight of a gang of poor youngsters in the picture window for whom we were giving a Christmas party. The big guy nearly collapsed and the last Ho-ho's didn't have much more force than a wheeze. But he carried it off. That was the very personal kind of concern I mean.

And out near the cottage I remember two farmers who hadn't spoken to each other for years. But when a fire took the barn of one of them, the other fixed it so they could both use his barn to milk the two herds. They still didn't speak, but the one who furnished the barn went through a tremendous amount of trouble and inconvenience to keep a neighbor in business.

Somebody asked him why he did it when they disliked each other so. And he said, "He was in trouble, he needed help, and I lived near him."

I chose Middlebury College because my father had gone there and because it was only eighteen miles from the cottage. Darned if I know which exerted the stronger force in reaching the decision. But I do know that being near the cottage came in handy and kept me out of trouble. Because when those periods of scholastic inactivity arrived—between the end of midyear exams and the beginning of the second semester, Easter recess, spring weekends with the baseball team out of town—I'd promptly head for the lake. And during summer vacations I spent at the lake all the time when I wasn't working.

In fact, one year my fraternity found itself embarrassingly short of furniture. We took a truck out to Addison and loaded it with what we needed from the cottage. We returned the furniture the following June. Nobody was inconvenienced, nobody needed it in between.

One year my roommate, Jack Dinkel, and I borrowed a cut-down Ford without mudguards and spent Easter vacation at the cottage. The lack of mudguards got us back to Middlebury in a pouring rain, unrecognizable and in no condition to attend our first class. But we had a fine time. And when we went somewhere at night we did deem it prudent to cut the motor and coast past the homes of any gossips who lived near the cottage; this way they wouldn't know what time we got home.

On two consecutive midyear breaks, Jack and I went out to Addison. One time we went out on snowshoes under the mistaken idea that going straight there across the fields instead of by road would cut down a tremendous amount on mileage. As a matter of fact we found out, the hard way, that it cut off at the most two miles, which still left sixteen to cover and the result nearly floored us. About the time, long after it got dark, that Jack fell getting across a fence and asked me to let him stay there and sleep awhile, I got really scared.

The other end-of-exams celebration was a trip to a dance out that way. After the dance we got a ride partway back to Middlebury. But from one o'clock to four in the morning we walked the rest of the way. And that, my friends, is a whole lot of walking after you've danced all the first part of the night.

In my senior year, when I had my mother's car at college, she wrote me and asked me to drive to the cottage and get *her* mother's wedding dress. It seemed that she wanted to wear it to a costume party.

The rule was very strict that you couldn't use a car anytime except during vacation without the dean's special permission. So I went up to his office.

"I wish to use the car to go out to our Lake Champlain cottage," I said.

"Oh, you do, do you," the dean said coldly. "Why do you wish to go out there?"

"My mother wants me to get my late grandmother's wedding dress for her," I said.

The dean leaned back and looked at me for a long time. "You say she wants you to get your grandmother's *wedding* dress for her?"

I said, "Yes, sir. You see she wants to wear it." I had begun to get a little nervous. He looked at me some more.

Finally he said, "Hoyt, I've said all year that if any student could face me with a completely new excuse, one that I hadn't ever heard before, I would let him use the car without—er—further ado. May I say that this is the most original excuse I've *ever* had presented to me. You have won the competition and—er—retired the trophy."

Mostly, though, the time I spent at the cottage during college, was during the summer vacations. We had no other home. Some of the time my mother was there, some of the time I was alone. She was teaching then, and her school always ended later than mine in the spring and began earlier in the fall.

When I arrived in June the first order of business, after the blinds were taken off and stowed away and the place swept out, was to clean off the swimming ledge.

The cottage could not boast a sand beach. The beach was made up of pieces of slate of various sizes. I realize that a beach made up of pieces of broken slate doesn't sound good at all for bare feet. But actually it wasn't as bad as it sounds. These pieces were flat, round, and incredibly smooth to the touch. The edges had all been worn smooth by the action of the water.

You could find round pieces of slate any size you wanted. You could write on them with another piece of slate. And they were perfect for skipping.

No matter what age or sex the person was to whom you showed the beach for the first time, that person would promptly gather a handful of slate stones and try to skip them. Some of these people were pretty inept at it, but they'd all try.

135

For children it was a regular fairyland: all those stones and nobody to tell you not to throw them into the water. All this and writing on them too. Kids would have picture-drawing contests, stone-skipping contests; they'd leave the beach only reluctantly, under protest.

All this slate came from the ledges that made up the cliff in front of our cottage and extended out into the water. It had been broken off by the action of the water, and by freezing and thawing.

But there was still a lot of ledge intact. And one especially wide, flat piece of it extended out from our beach, diagonally. It extended beyond a person's depth.

The winter would leave stones on it, and a good husky north wind in summer would bring others. By spending considerable time cleaning these off when we arrived in June, we'd have a smooth—almost a cement-smooth—surface for swimming. It would be slippery to start with, but when a lot of people were using it several times a day, this slickness would wear off quickly. Then, with a few minutes of re-cleaning after each north wind, it would stay clean. We considered ourselves very lucky to have the ledge. This ledge remains intact today and we still use it for swimming, the only one of its kind I know about.

Once while I was alone there in the fall, I came out one morning to look down from the cliff at the beach. Something which I took to be a big log had drifted in during the night.

I went around and down the path and the stairs to the beach. And when I got down there I found that it was not a log but a huge fish. It was between five and six feet long, and very dead. It must have weighed over a hundred pounds. It had an uneven tail, like a shark's, the top segment longer than the bottom one.

Its mouth was underneath like a shark's, set back about eight inches from the end of its snout. But where a shark's mouth is a half-moon in shape with a lot of teeth, this one was small and round and had no teeth at all. It had a cartilage ring around the perimeter of its mouth. And when I got the ice tongs and tried to drag it out of the water by hooking one prong of the tongs in its mouth, I found that the cartilage ring was attached to a round membrane tube that pulled out about eight inches. We theorized later that the fish could extend this tube and use it like a vacuum cleaner to suck things up from places it couldn't get its head into.

I had never seen anything like it in Lake Champlain and certainly never anything that big. Dr. Phelps, a neighbor, came along about that time and he was as astonished by the fish as I was. He went for his camera and also for someone to snap a picture, because it was going to take both of us to lift the thing.

We hooked the ice tongs securely in its mouth, and ran a thick stick through the handles of the tongs. Then, with one of us on each end of the stick, we lifted the fish.

It became apparent immediately that, even with holding the stick as high as we could, the fish's tail would drag on the ground. So we found a place where two sizable rocks were close together. We climbed up on the two rocks, then lifted the fish and again held him as high as we could. That time his tail cleared the ground and the pictures were snapped.

Dr. Phelps had a relative who had spent most of the summer at Potash Bay. Most of each day he had sat out in a boat fishing for bass with live bait. His success had been definitely mediocre. Dr. Phelps had an enlargement of the picture made and he sent it to this friend. The covering message said, "Just as soon as you left, look what we caught."

Naturally we wanted to know what kind of fish it was, but we were hampered by the condition of what might be called the remains. When we had been taking the picture everybody connected with the affair had had to hold his breath. That fish was really ripe. We showed it to as many people as we could get to come there to the beach. But in less than an hour the fish's olfactory condition had deteriorated to a marked degree. And after a hasty council of war we towed the fish far out into the lake and sank him.

However, by showing the pictures and by describing the fish and answering questions, an expert whom we consulted was convinced that our fish had been a mud sturgeon.

The sturgeon had had a swollen and bloody vent and the expert theorized that a stomach blow had been the cause of his demise. The blow might have been from a ship's propeller, the man said.

"This fish gives us one explanation of the Lake Champlain Monster that people claim to have seen from time to time. If about three fish of this size broached the surface between you and the setting sun, in line, you'd swear you'd seen a huge sea serpent."

I don't know whether Dr. Phelps ever told his relative the truth about our fish. But if he didn't, that friend must have been a really frustrated fisherman.

In the years while I was in college, and a few years before and after college, Rob Moorby, owner of the meadow and pasture land that bordered the cottage on three sides, sold off his lakeshore in building lots. At the back of all these lots (and ours) he fenced off an access road servicing all of them. You drove along this road, and you no longer had to open and close a gate. We now began to have neighbors; that was how Dr. Phelps and the others who came to see the fish reached the beach so quickly.

These new summer residents were very pleasant people. It wasn't the lonely and remote place it had been, but my mother, for one, was glad of it. Always she had been afraid to stay down there alone. Now that there were neighbors she didn't mind as much.

About this time, too, I brushed a couple of times against a fallacy that was everywhere being subscribed to unthinkingly by people who vacationed near any lake. The fallacy was that when you tipped over, or for some other reason found yourself in trouble in the water, you took your trousers off at once to get rid of the weight.

Everybody had heard that this was the thing to do; everybody was impressed. Novels had people doing it. News stories said, "Of course the first thing the victim did was rid himself of his trousers."

It was probably pretty good advice at that, *if* your situation demanded it. But to do this when, for instance, help was only a few hundred yards away, when you were in no trouble at all, was rank stupidity and would cost you a pair of pants. But because it was the thing to do, people did it with no thought whatever. And my two brushes with it were this type of automatic reaction.

Among our new neighbors was one who had a sailboat. He went out in a north wind and tipped over. He and his wife were okay and could cling to the boat until help came. But you were supposed to take off your pants: and he took off his pants. He handed them to his wife while he swam for pieces of gear, and she somehow lost them.

So when we got the man and his wife—and the boat (getting the boat required some doing, believe me)—the enormity of his trouble was immediately outlined for us.

In the pocket of those pants he had been carrying his two hundred fifty dollars of vacation money.

We rallied around and helped in any way we could. I lent him the money to telegraph for more funds. We searched the beach in each direction every morning for weeks, looking for those pants. Remember, this was in the days before skin-diving.

I believe he had to cut his vacation short because of depletion of funds, but we looked every day the rest of the summer. And for years afterward I never saw a piece of heavy cloth washed up on the beach without examining it thoroughly to make sure it wasn't those pants.

Shortly after our neighbor's mishap I sat one late dusk on the porch, working out the details of a story in my mind. It was one of those breathlessly still evenings that we get sometimes, and I could hear a fast motorboat out toward the middle of the lake. I paid little attention to it.

All of a sudden the motor ran free, as if the propeller had come out of water, and then cut off.

In a moment or so I heard the cry *Help!* coming faintly across the water. It was repeated almost at once, and that time I was sure I had heard it right. It went on in a fairly regular cadence.

I ran to a nearby cottage and got Malcolm Wright. He listened and heard it too. We ran for the beach and launched my canoe-skiff. No one had a motor who was living there then; it was still fairly early in the history of motors, and we ourselves had had that bad experience with the first one, which I've described earlier.

I rowed and Malcolm paddled in the stern. We gave it everything we had. The canoe-skiff flew.

Every little while we'd stop and listen; the calls still came. When we came even with Oven Point, an outboard motor started up there. He stayed even with us for the rest of the race out across the water. You couldn't do that against an outboard today, but we did it then.

For a while the cries seemed just as far away as they ever had. And I'll confess I entertained the thought that somebody was playing a practical joke and moving away as fast as we came on. If that were the case I planned to catch him and mess him up some if I could.

We were by that time in the middle of the lake, almost two miles from our beach. We heard another motor start up at Mullen Brook on the New York side. This sounded like a faster motor than the one we had been keeping abreast of.

140

About two-thirds of the way across, things came to a climax rapidly. We reached the people in the water, the boat from Mullen Brook reached them, and the boat from Oven Point arrived moments later. The boat from Mullen Brook had a searchlight, and we had a flash.

There were three people in the water, two men and a girl, and no boat. Either they had left it, or the weight of the motor had sunk it. We circled them, we talked back and forth. They were from the New York side, so we decided to help all three of them into the boat from Mullen Brook, since doing so would save the other Vermont boat and mine from going clear to New York.

Neither of the men in the water had any pants on.

"Of course we took our pants off," one of them explained.

And if there ever was a situation where this was the correct procedure, here it was. Except for one thing. Both young men had great big thick sweaters on that would have been twice as heavy, wet, as a pair of summer trousers. But it had never occurred to them to take the heavy sweaters off and leave the pants on. When in trouble you took off your pants.

We got them loaded into the Mullen Brook boat, and the man from Oven Point asked us what kind of a motor we were using. I said an Armstrong Motor, thinking I was joking. But it was very dark and he said it must be a good make; very quiet too. So after that I figured it was best just to glide off to one side and start for home.

On the way home Malcolm and I talked about what had happened and felt very good indeed. We felt very virtuous, but I don't believe that was the whole thing. Everybody needs an occasional high moment of effort and adventure. We'd had such a moment, and were extremely contented as a result. People "made over" us when we got back. We told our story, showed our blisters. And all in all we basked in admiration's light.

141

It was just another example of how the cottage, during my college years, furnished the excitement and adventure that I needed. Excitement and adventure that might have led me into trouble if the cottage—with its fishing, swimming, sturgeon-finding, rescues—hadn't filled the need so admirably when things grew dull at school.

12

By No Means Big League

In my youth we didn't have television with all its blessings, and so did not have baseball's Game of the Week or Monday Night Baseball to sit and watch on the boob tube. How then did we satisfy without them the baseball craving which most of us surely had?

The nearest big-league parks were Fenway Park and Braves Field in Boston; Montreal didn't have a major-league team yet. Some of us saw games in Boston or New York once every couple of years. Most of us never saw any big-league games at all because, frankly, we couldn't afford the trip. Yet all the male youth followed big-league baseball far closer than they do today. Many of my friends knew every batting average in either league.

At World Series time huge simulated baseball diamonds would be mounted on the front of newspaper-office buildings and a ball, manipulated by rubber bands, would dutifully make each play as the results reached the newspaper office by telegraph. The crowds in front of these "play-o-graphs" were gigantic; streets had to be closed off. And newspaper extras hit the streets minutes after the game ended.

Perhaps this was because there was still no professional football or basketball, so our allegiance wasn't divided. Certainly every kid played baseball himself. You played whether you had four at the vacant lot that day or twenty-four. If it was a small number you played One-o'-Cat, if it was a large number you played a regular game. There aren't many vacant lots now—playgrounds, yes, but no vacant lots. And parents are everywhere, organizing. No parent ever came near our baseball games except to take you by the ear and lead you home when you were late for supper. Even leading a transgressor home by the ear has disappeared from the scene today.

At the cottage we were hampered by lack of numbers, there being mostly only two of us. But we'd go over the fence into Moorby's pasture and play Hit-the-Bat, a game which, as I look back on it, furnished a terrific amount of fielding practice. In Hit-the-Bat, the batter hits to the other player or players and then lays the bat down at right angles to the spot where the ball landed. From that spot the other player tries to hit the bat with his return throw. If he succeeds, he becomes the hitter, and the former hitter takes his place in the field.

All this took care of the kids nicely. But what about the adults who watch television baseball now?

Well, the best of them played in amateur and semi-pro leagues every Sunday and every holiday all spring and summer and early fall. And all the rest of them went to the games and followed the fortunes of the home team.

There were literally thousands of these teams all over the United States. Some of them were wonderful, some were mediocre, and some were incredibly bad. They represented cities, towns, industrial companies, even villages so small their total male population was hardly more than nine. They didn't spend their time *watching* really good baseball, they spent their time *playing* mediocre or bad baseball. They must have been wrong, because almost all these teams and their leagues have folded for lack of spectators or players or both. Some of the players have been lost to softball, some sit in front of the TV sets and see first-rank teams perform. But while all this was going on we actually had a pretty wonderful time playing or watching live baseball.

By the time I finished college I was collecting an amazing variety of rejection slips from a variety of publications, all of which protested vehemently that there was no lack of merit in what I had written: the magazines or publishers just weren't able to take advantage of the terrific opportunity I had given them to buy. In turn there began to dawn on me the quiet suspicion that they lied in their teeth.

Since I had developed a habit of eating as a very small child and hated to break myself of it, I took a job coaching Waterville High School in central New York until such time as editorial attitudes or my ability should change.

I played shortstop for the Waterville town team till school was dismissed each year. Then I came up to the cottage to write for the summer. But I loved baseball.

The West Addison town team approached me and asked if I would play with them the first Sunday I was back. They had a game with the neighboring town of Panton to the north. With the excellent Waterville team in mind I accepted at once.

Immediately I ran into trouble at home. My mother did not think I should play ball on Sunday. This developed into a major running argument that lasted for years. For my part I promised to go to church every Sunday in the morning if I could play in the afternoon.

My mother said, "You have six days to play ball. Why do you have to play on Sunday?"

And my answer was, "*I* can play the other six days of the week, but none of the rest of the team can. You can't play ball alone."

On Sunday I got a rude awakening. Panton proceeded to take West Addison apart. The West Addison team had no uniforms and the pitcher either walked the men who faced him or grooved the ball and had it creamed. Now and then a pop fly would come out which would, as like as not, be dropped or staggered around under and missed. It was just incredible. We couldn't get anybody out except at rare intervals. Once I made every out in an inning, but in between those three chances that came my way, Panton scored six runs.

I suggested a new pitcher. There was little difference. All this was taking time. At shortstop I began to call for every pop fly in the infield and some in the short outfield. But outs were still hard to come by, and errors mounted almost as fast as the Panton runs.

We tried other pitchers with little luck. Finally, along about the seventh inning, I went in to pitch.

By no stretch of the imagination was I a pitcher. Ordinarily wild horses couldn't have dragged me to the mound. But by then we had found we had no pitcher left who could throw the ball over the plate except by accident. The parade of walked batters was discouraging and boring. Even the Panton players didn't enjoy walking, one after another. Some of the team had to get home for chores and I had to get home for supper. At least I could throw straight. All spring I had been pitching batting practice for my high-school boys.

I had no real fast ball except what I called a Thespian fast ball: by play-acting, I'd make the pitch sneaky fast. I had a good out-drop. By throwing with a lot of motion I could change this to a *slow* out-drop. I had a little wrinkle of an in-curve (today's slider) and a wide roundhouse sidearm out-curve.

The pitchers who preceded me had had nothing but

145

speed. This reacted to my advantage by keeping everybody off balance. The fact that Panton had only three innings to get used to my slow stuff also was in my favor. I pitched pretty well but could do nothing about the errors behind me except hope for strikeouts or rollers to the box.

I finished the game and was only scored on a couple of times. The one thing I remember was the Panton player who took two full swings at one pitch. I fired what I laughingly called my fast ball at him and then, with all kinds of facial expressions of supreme effort, gave him the slow ball. He swung once as it approached the plate, jerked the bat back and swung again after the ball was nicely past him. I've seen players out ahead of a pitch, but never before or since have I seen anybody strike twice at one pitch.

That ended the West Addison baseball team. On Monday evening Dick Smith, the manager of Panton, came down to the cottage.

"We'd like to have you play with us," he said.

I said I had agreed to play with West Addison. I didn't add that I was kicking myself all over the place for having made such a promise.

"I hear they're giving up," Dick said. "They got discouraged Sunday."

I assured him that if that was true, I'd be glad to play for Panton.

"Good," Dick said. "We take up a collection at our games. We'll pay you whenever the collection warrants it."

Thus began a relationship that lasted until I was forty-four years old. It is dramatized a bit if I tell you that Dick Smith had been recently married when I joined the Panton team. He played behind me in center field. Before I hung up my glove his two sons were playing second base and first base beside me in the infield. After I retired, the young man who took my place was less than

adequate and at Dick's request I came back and played one more season when I was forty-six, while he looked for another shortstop.

Why then do I feel that it was better to have played all those years of mediocre baseball than to have watched somebody else play much better ball? Why would a staid writer and businessman spend every summer Sunday afternoon and every summer holiday afternoon for all those years, his skinny legs encased in short pants, playing a game? Why would he have looked forward to those games all week, have hardly been able to wait for Sunday afternoon? Why would he have spent hours each week practicing after dinner, and have spent more hours talking over the games?

Darned if I know for sure. Maybe it was the excitement of competition, maybe it was the plaudits of the crowd, maybe it was the thrill of winning, maybe a combination of those things and others. Maybe it was this real head-to-head physical competition that I mentioned, and which they say man needs. Anyhow, it was that way. Perhaps if I tell you some of the highlights of those years you'll begin to understand a little better.

First there were the people you played with, the personnel of the Panton team. You were very loyal to them and they to you. You got so you knew what to expect of them. Some of the younger ones came and went, but there was a nucleus of five or six of us that played for many years with the team.

One was the catcher. He was the smallest catcher I ever saw. They'd hit him coming in from third when he tried to block the plate and he'd fly through the air like a bag of bones. Mostly he held on to the ball.

Dick Smith would grit his teeth and stand there and get hit to get on base. He seemed contemptuous of any effort to make it look authentic; he never put on an act of trying to get out of the way. He just stood there and got hit, preferably on the shoulder. And sometimes with a

148

speedball pitcher in there, it must have hurt like crazy. Sometimes he was so obvious about it that the ump would not give him first base. But he never changed in this matter through all the years I played with him.

We had two third basemen during my tenure at shortstop, Brooks and Sunderland. They were both excellent ballplayers. Brooks was the more flamboyant; Sunderland was very steady.

Brooks and I figured up all sorts of things to get people out. For instance, with a runner on third base, Brooks would yell to our pitcher, "Watch out for the bunt!" On the first pitch he would charge in toward the plate. The man on third, seeing he wasn't being held on, would move in nearly as far as Brooks went.

If he moved in, Brooks would yell the same thing on the second pitch, and again make his charge toward the plate. The base-runner, made bold by the previous play, would usually follow Brooks farther down the baseline that time. Meantime, with the pitch I would break for third base from shortstop. The catcher would throw for the base and I would tag the runner out as he tried to scramble back to safety.

Obviously this would only work once with each team. Even if you didn't play them again for a couple of years, you could never use it again. We'd use it once or twice a year when new teams came down from Burlington to play us.

Another time Brooks was having a bad afternoon. Everybody has one once in a while. He'd field perfectly, but then he'd throw over the first baseman's head. After the error, he got to thinking about each throw, and this made it worse. He threw wild every time.

In the last inning a ball was hit hard to third and Brooks gobbled it up. I had broken to my right with the hit, but, when I saw where the ball was headed, had stopped and was just standing there watching.

Brooks never hesitated. He whirled and threw the

ball at me. Flabbergasted, I snapped my hands up, caught it, made the pivot and threw to first. We got the man easily. Brooks had simply figured that if he couldn't throw a ball across the diamond straight that day, I could.

When we came in to the bench Dick Smith took a very dim view of the maneuver.

"You guys start clowning around, you'll lose us a ball game."

But I'm sincerely convinced that Brooks hadn't been clowning. He'd made what he considered to be the play with the best chance of getting the out. You might not be expecting what he would think up to do, but it was always aimed at getting somebody out.

Our first baseman ran a farm. He must have done a lot of wood-chopping in his time because he could meet the ball absolutely dead center. He hit an awful lot of line drives. The second baseman ran an orchard. He was very quiet, the opposite of Brooks. He was an infield DiMaggio. He expended exactly the amount of energy needed to get to the ball and field it. Never anything fancy. But when you thought it over afterward, nobody could have got the job done better or even as well.

Four pitchers I remember particularly through the years. The catcher's cousin was one. He had coached a big high school for years and was very old for playing ball, but was very cagey and hard to hit. There was Louis Walters, a black man, extremely efficient; Ron MacIntyre, a barber who was unhittable when he was right; and Jerry Hatch, a farmer just out of high school.

When any of the four of them was on the mound, life was very pleasant for an infielder. Nobody who hasn't played a lot of ball understands about this. When a pitcher is in control, nobody hits the ball square. Balls come bouncing to the infielders on nice easy hops. The pop-flies give you time to get under them.

But when a pitcher doesn't have much stuff, you get

150

wicked grass-cutters that handcuff you, pop-flies are blooped over the infielder's heads, everything is hard and just out of your reach. You can have a pretty miserable afternoon.

Some of the men I played against were noteworthy too. I played in the same league with Hal Schumacher at Waterville, before he starred for the then New York Giants. Hal played for the Dolgeville team. And playing for Panton I hit against Ray Fischer, the old big-league pitcher for the Yankees. He was the baseball coach at the University of Michigan and spent his summers on the lake. He pitched some for Vergennes.

Boy, was he something to face! I drove the ball to the outfield the first time I was up. But there were men on base the second time I faced him and he struck me out on three sizzling pitched balls. He may have been old but he could still rise to the occasion completely.

I also played against a couple of Burlington men who are still umpiring college games. I see them every year when I watch Middlebury College play.

On holidays, sometimes the meat of the Panton team were hired to play for other towns. In such cases Panton didn't schedule a game, and four or five of us would appear in some other line-up. Bridport had a yearly Old Home Day and usually hired us. I played for Middlebury too. I got two for three that day, and they tried to hire me regularly. I stuck with Panton as being nearer the cottage.

Once when we were playing for Bridport the catcher from Chappy Johnson's All Stars, a traveling black team that I had seen perform a couple of times, was hired to play with us.

At that time blacks did not play with the big leagues, and many who were of big-league caliber traveled around playing town teams. They would put on a real show, getting a couple of quick runs on a flurry of solid hits. Then, unexplainably, all their efforts would produce high fly balls to the outfielders. Thus they'd always win by a couple of runs, and the local team wouldn't be disgraced—would actually be very proud of having held them down—and would book them again.

One time I heard some hecklers calling to Chappy Johnson himself. "Hey, Chappy, how many hits you got?" they yelled, knowing that he had hit several long outs to the outfield.

Chappy called back: "Mo' than you have. Yes sir, mo' than you have."

Playing with Johnson's catcher, who was probably good enough to have played with almost any big-league team, was an experience.

Early in the game a fast opponent took a big lead and tried to steal second on the first pitch. The batter was a righthander, so it was up to the second baseman to cover, and not me.

The throw was so hard and quick that the pitcher had to duck, and our second baseman barely made it to the bag in time to catch the throw. When he did catch it in his glove he put the glove on the first-base side of second so the runner would have to slide into the ball.

He waited a few seconds. Then he looked up to see why nobody was arriving.

The reason was plain enough. The runner had been only nicely started on his trip when the ball arrived at its destination. Horrified, he had done the only thing he could do: he turned back toward first. The time during which our infielder had waited for his slide, plus the incredibly short distance he had covered, allowed him to make it back safely to first.

We weren't used to catchers who could throw like that.

Once a minor-league pitcher from the Louisville, Kentucky, team played one game with us in right field. Boy, did *he* have a rifle arm! One man hit a hard grounder between the first and second basemen, a good solid base hit. Then he loafed just a little going to first; no sense killing himself on a sure hit that couldn't be stretched into a double.

The pitcher, playing right field for us, fielded the ball cleanly on a dead run and blasted a throw to first that caught the runner by a step. It also nearly de-handed the shocked first baseman. That was the only time in all the years I played ball that I ever saw a right-fielder throw out a man running from home to first base.

There were, too, the little incidents that happened over the years. Hundreds of them. The first time my sister-in-law, Catherine McPhee, came to visit us at the cottage and went with us Sunday afternoon to the ball game, the earliest arrivals were members of the team intent on batting practice. We parked behind the backstop where Catherine and Marg, my wife, could watch comfortably from the car.

When we ran out on the field we spooked up a rabbit from around the area of second base. He took off across the outfield: it must have shaken him some to have a bunch of humans fan out toward him with huge gloves on. What he had been hiding behind I never knew, because there didn't seem to be anything out there high enough.

Catherine took this very big indeed. For years afterward she would tell people about the time her brother-in-law's team ran out on to the field—"and I know you won't believe this, but a full-grown rabbit ran out of the infield."

Our daughter, Margie, was born on a Saturday in July 1933, and I played ball on Sunday, going to the hospital in Middlebury before and after the game. Afterward a number of friends came to Marg and told her that I grinned all through the game and seemed almost to be dancing in every move I made out there at shortstop.

One of my sisters-in-law, Marion, was at the cottage

at the time and she looked very much like Marg. She went to Sunday's game with me. All the following week I heard rumors that Marg Hoyt had given birth to a baby girl on Saturday and had been at the ball game Sunday with Murray.

There was a pitcher living in Middlebury, Frannie Corvin, who was in my opinion the best pitcher in Addison County, perhaps in the state. I played with him a few times when we were hired by the same team, and against him a whole lot of times. Once, playing for Bridport, we played the first game of a double-header which was to feature Middlebury *vs* the Howe Scale Company in the second game.

Frannie shut out the team we were playing against, 6–0. We started to watch the second game and the Middlebury pitcher was hit hard in the first inning. With two runs already scored against them, and nobody out, they hastily came to Frannie and hired him to pitch the rest of the game.

Mind you, he had pitched nine innings: but he went in and pitched nine more without being scored on. The final score was 2–0, both of those runs given up by the first pitcher. Once in a while, on his mail route, he used to hang up his mailbag on the backstop and pitch fifteen minutes or so of batting practice for Middlebury College at the request of the coach. The coach used to like to show his team now and then what it was like to face real pitching.

Once in an Addison County League game, Ripton hired Frannie to pitch against Panton. Ripton had deliberately sacrificed a man on their league roster and put Frannie on in case they might sometime find him without a Sunday game and be able to hire him. This struck Dick Smith as dirty pool.

But he rose to the occasion. He went to Middlebury Saturday night, found Frannie, and bought him beer after beer until nearly morning.

154

By No Means Big League

The next afternoon in Ripton, Frannie had trouble the first couple of innings. Several times he fell off the mound. But this didn't last, or keep Frannie from burning the ball across the plate. Even a mildly impaired Frannie was an awesome thing. Unfortunately his infield and outfield let him down just often enough for us to win.

And in that game, played up in the mountains, there were black flies. Black flies do things to me. I felt a bite under the roll of my pants leg. In the excitement of the game I brushed at it. I did this over and over. When I took off my uniform after the game, there was the black fly, dead but half buried in my leg. The leg began to swell that night, and I spent three or four days the next week immobile, my leg up on a chair.

Panton played its home games in Clayt Curler's pasture. This took care of mowing; it was done automatically for us. It caused one other problem which had to be taken care of with a shovel and cart and a liberal sprinkling of sawdust.

Cars parked along the first-base side of the diamond. On the third-base side there was a stone ledge, which made very effective natural bleachers. Teams from Burlington used to sneer openly at our set up.

They were right. But it was wonderful compared to some we played on. Still, during the years I played ball I did get to play on some of the finest ball diamonds in the state. Centennial Field, the University of Vermont's plant in Burlington, was one of these; the Middlebury College diamond was another. Mostly these fields were used for league play-offs.

Actually you had to be a much better infielder to do well on the various town diamonds than you did to play well in these immaculate super-parks. All bounces were predictable in them, but in Clayt Curler's pasture you sidled in on grounders suspiciously, ready for anything.

Then there was the time I made the most frightening offer I ever made.

A Yale football tackle married into our area and tried out for the Panton team. Unfortunately his football skill didn't transfer over into baseball, and he held me personally responsible as captain for our refusal of his services. But Dick did ask him to umpire on bases.

I got on first. Routinely the pitcher tried to pick me off, routinely I got back. Routinely the first baseman swung around and touched me, seconds late. Routinely he threw back to the pitcher.

We started to go on with the game; the pitcher got his sign and was about to pitch. But all the time this Yale man was making a big noise next to first base, waving his arms. Finally he got everybody to look at him. It seemed he had called me out on that last play and nobody had paid any attention to him because it had never occurred to anybody that I was out.

I was hopping mad; the red hair stood up on the back of my neck. I left first base and in the heat of the moment I made my offer. I offered to lick this member of Yale's varsity line.

We stood there, our chins stuck out, jawing at each other, all 150 pounds of me, all 240 pounds of him. I'd start away, think of something else that needed saying, turn and say it.

Suddenly I became aware that he was looking over my shoulder instead of at me. I turned and the entire Panton bench and most of the spectators were coming across the field led by Dick Smith, purpose showing in every movement. It was a regular wave of irate farmers and townspeople.

The rhubarb lasted for some time. It was finally compromised by my losing first base and another man coming in to umpire. When I began to think clearly again, the magnitude of my offer overwhelmed me. For years afterward I have been thankful he did not take me up on it: I'd have been a red-headed grease spot if he had.

What were the two or three plays I remember best? Well, first on the negative side, there was the afternoon at Vergennes when I made four or five errors. It was the most horrible day of my baseball life.

We had sixty dollars riding on the outcome, a winner-take-gate-receipts setup. Vergennes had covered the skinned part of the infield with new soft loam, then rolled it. On the first hard-hit grounder to me, I put my glove where the ball should have been. It went under my glove, hit my leg, and the man was safe. It happened right off again. It kept happening.

Catching hard grounders is a reflex action. And due to the soft loam the grounders weren't coming off the ground as high as my reflexes said they should. I was messing them up.

I felt worse than I ever had before or have since in a game. My teammates were wonderful; nobody upbraided me, everybody expressed sympathy and confidence. Still, I felt awful.

I got a couple of grounders in between errors, but I still made errors. Finally, when I saw that I couldn't handle the hard ones off the soft loam, I moved in almost to the baseline where I could take the hops off the grass. I finished the game this way. Better to have my range to each side cut 'way down, than to go on missing chances. This worked fairly well. But the damage was done. We lost the game and the sixty dollars because of my errors. It was a debacle for me, the most complete one I ever had.

There was the other side of the coin, though. One time with Louis Walters pitching, somebody knocked a very high foul which seemed due to come down behind third base and on top of that ledge I spoke of. Louis glanced up, saw where it was going, got a new ball from the umpire (who was working behind the pitcher the way they often did in our games because of the lack of protective equipment) and prepared to pitch again to the hitter. But he found that the catcher and the hitter both were standing there looking over at the ledge. So he looked too.

I had run to the foot of the ledge. There I had to take my eyes off the ball, because the footing was terrible. I leaped from outcropping to outcropping partway up the ledge, glanced up, saw I wasn't far enough, leaped forward some more.

I glanced up again and the ball was there. I stuck out my glove and the ball stayed in the glove.

Louis gave the new ball back to the umpire and received the old one from me when I leaped down off the ledge.

But the play that meant the most to me and to the team came in a play-off for the league championship against Shelburne on Centennial Field before a very large crowd.

It was a tight game, we led 1–0. Shelburne had a player who was hitting over .400, a big broad-shouldered man who really slammed the ball. We had held him down pretty well in that game, but you couldn't hold him down for long.

We were in trouble in the last half of the ninth inning. With two out they had men on second and third base, which might be the tying and winning runs. The .400 hitter was up, and if he hit safely those two men would score and we'd lose the game. If we got him out, we'd win. It was that simple.

He hit a screamer that passed just to the third-base side of the pitcher's head. I started with the crack of the bat. I got over a few steps, saw I wasn't going to make it; I launched myself parallel to the ground, my arms extended.

I felt the ball hit the glove. I concentrated so much on hanging on that I landed on my face and chest and stomach with no arms or elbows available to break the fall.

But I hung on. We were league champions.

So this is my explanation of why I feel we had more fun playing mediocre baseball than we would have had watching first-class ball on television. The small leagues are mostly gone and a lot of people sit indoors on a lovely Sunday afternoon watching the tube and going to the refrigerator for a beer during the commercials. It's more comfortable, less work. But I personally had more fun the old way.

When I think of all those confrontations, of the people I played with and against, of the hundreds and hundreds of exciting and interesting things that happened, I'd still jump at the chance to do it over again. My head is bloody but unbowed.

13

Hunting Ducks

A lot of people can't say enough scathing things about hunters. For their money, hunters are great big bullies going around shooting defenseless animals for sport; killing for pleasure, and frothing at the mouth in their lust for blood.

Well, there are hunters and hunters. I'm not going to work up a defense for the moneyed characters who hunt big game for trophy heads, who maybe hire a lot of beaters, and whose guides aim the gun and do everything but pull the trigger for them. This type is strictly on their own in trying to change their image. Maybe they've got a good story; I wouldn't know. At least they provide a living for beaters and guides and outfitters. But like I say, if they want to defend themselves, they'd best be about it on their own behalf.

I would, however, like to say a few words on behalf of the 95 percent or better of little-guy hunters who couldn't need less either a rhinoceros head on their 8-x-15-foot living-room wall or a grizzly-skin rug on the floor in front of their non-existent fireplace. What these everyday hunters need, quite simply, is food. Meat on the table.

If they're successful they eat pheasant or partridge, or even deer steaks. If they're unsuccessful they eat what the budget offers and this in more cases than a few is baked beans or macaroni or some such. As for blood lust, they don't give the most insignificant hoot whether a professional butcher does the killing and preparing, or whether they do it themselves. Except that when they do it themselves it's more or less free, and when the professional butcher does it it costs an arm or a leg per pound. The animal is just as dead either way.

These run-of-the-mill hunters don't really need the food? That's not what I hear from my friends who hunt. Probably they wouldn't starve without it, but it sure upgrades their table and allows room in the budget for a whole lot of extras, including maybe a bottle of champagne on New Year's Eve. And a bottle of champagne New Year's Eve could have all sorts of interesting side effects.

And if hunting upgrades the table in this day of unemployment insurance, social security, food stamps, welfare, just think what it must have meant to the little character who lost his job or fell upon hard times back in the 1930's when my generation was fighting an often losing war with the world; and there was that dilly-lou of a Depression riding roughshod up and down the land clipping little guys right and left. So you lost your job. So you were hungry. So get yourself some food.

And that's what millions of us did. We took our

trusty twelve-gauge in hand and went after game—food —and you'd be amazed at how little it would have worried us to have had people call us bloodthirsty.

I brought my bride home to the cottage on Lake Champlain on July 17, 1932. We had been married July 16 in Elmira, New York. We came to the cottage because there was no rent, there was a garden, there was a lake full of fish. There was ice and milk and an occasional bee tree full of honey. I've told about these matters.

My mother took an extended trip to the Rockies and the National Parks so we could have the cottage to ourselves. We always said that we came directly to the cottage and my mother took our wedding trip for us. The Great Depression had the United States by the throat. I personally by then was trying to make it full-time as a free-lance writer and, as I've said, editors were not always overwhelmed by the excellence of my efforts.

In other words, I had ambition, a job, but no regular pay check. I had to cut my expenses back below any checks that came in. I had two mouths to feed instead of just one. And as long as there were edible fish, animals, birds, I intended to feed those two mouths.

Fall and the hunting season came not a moment too soon. Fish is a fine food and I love it. But after a couple of months of it we began to wonder if we might grow scales and fins.

When duck season opened, Bill Burpee and I got up while it was still dark and drove down through the fields and flats of the Burpee farm which bordered Dead Creek, an area of potholes and cattails that drains finally (and imperceptibly) into Lake Champlain via Otter Creek.

When it got light enough to see, we worked our way carefully and noiselessly—we hoped—through cattails taller than we were, out toward one of those potholes. Bill knew where the potholes were; which was a good thing, because from the banks of the creek the whole territory looked like a solid green expanse of waving

161

cattails with no water anywhere. Only when you started to wade through those cattails did you find that you were wading in half a foot or more of water all the time. It was only where the water got deeper, too deep for cattails to grow, that the potholes existed.

We approached the pothole with extreme caution. We knew there were ducks present because we could hear them splashing and quacking. We reached the edge of the open water. We peered carefully through the last few cattails. Nothing was in sight anywhere. Yet we could hear the quacking and the splashing going on merrily all the while.

"They must be just out of sight," Bill whispered next to my ear, "in the shallower water at the edge of the cattails."

We waited for them to come out and get shot. They didn't come. They talked a lot and splashed even more. But the getting-shot bit didn't seem to appeal to them.

We began to grow impatient. Finally Bill whispered, "Let's sneak up on them. If we scare them and they fly we might get a shot. Anyway we couldn't be any worse off than we are just standing here."

So we started to wade laboriously around the perimeter of the pothole toward the sounds of duck merriment. Did you ever try to wade noiselessly through half a foot of water among seven-foot cattails that swish and rustle alarmingly every time you touch them? It's an experience, believe me. It was chilly and we'd been shivering when we entered the cattails. We got over that quickly: in our heavy clothing we began to sweat profusely.

We strained and looked, moved forward, strained and looked again. But we never did quite get our eyes on the ducks. Almost, you understand, but not quite. Yet neither did they fly. We kept pressing forward, realizing that sounds seem sometimes deceptively close.

After considerable of this we came to a place where

a small army had moved through the cattails. We stopped and looked at it. The path was much, much too wide, and the area much too disturbed, to have been the work of ducks.

As we stood there thinking about it and examining it, the place began to have a familiar look. We seemed to have seen it before.

Bill whispered, "I think this must be where we came in in the first place. Those so-and-so ducks must have known all along about our being here. They've been keeping just ahead of us clear around the perimeter of the pothole."

"Don't be silly," I whispered back.

But a little further examination convinced both of us.

Bill said, "Let's crash right at them fast and make them fly. We may get a shot that way."

So we crashed right at them fast. Nothing happened. We stopped and listened. Now the sounds of splashing were on all sides of us. Obviously we had succeeded in scattering the ducks but not in making them fly.

We tried some more. We failed miserably. We finally gave up and waded out along the path we had made in entering the cattails. With all that water in among all those cattails those ducks could have gone on playing that game in perfect safety as long as we wanted to play it with them. Defenseless? Hah!

We went home from that expedition empty-handed. I don't know what Bill ate in place of ducks, but I think Marg and I ate beans. Well, you lose some, you win some.

As autumn progresses, more and more ducks come into Lake Champlain. The black ducks, teal and wood ducks that have nested in Dead Creek and other local swamp areas, take to rafting up out toward the middle of the lake as soon as hunting season starts. With a whole lot of characters like Burpee and Hoyt crashing around

163

in the cattails of their nesting areas, they learn to leave the swamps before it gets light in the mornings and they don't return until after dusk at night. They sit out there and sleep all day, and they come into the swamp areas where the food is, to feed all night.

In contrast to the native ducks, which are staying on for a while near where they were born, the migratory ducks from Canada start down the Lake Champlain flyway on their way south. It's hard to generalize, but there are two main varieties that come down: the whistlers, and the bluebills. There are mergansers of several kinds, canvasbacks, mallards, coot, helldivers, and many others. But the whistlers, or goldeneyes, seem to pass through the lake in the greatest numbers.

However, the bluebills come first. They've pretty well left the lake by the time the whistlers get that far south.

There is one orthodox way and a lot of unorthodox ways to get migratory ducks. The one orthodox method is with decoys and a blind. You build a wooden framework and then cover the outside with cedars, which are the main evergreen on the lake. You place this close to the water's edge. Inside you have a seat, and over the seat a cedar-covered roof to protect you when it rains. In front of the seat is an uncovered open space where you can rise up suddenly from behind the low front wall of the blind and shoot at the ducks when they drop in among, or fly over, your decoys. When you are seated you are hidden by the front-wall cedars that stick up, yet you can see the ducks coming by as you look out through the tops of the cedars or through peepholes in the sides of the blind.

It sounds pretty open-and-shut, pretty easy, the way I tell it. Unfortunately it isn't all that open-and-shut. Unexpected things happen. In fact the ratio of unexpected things to expected things is about nine to one.

Just a few quick examples. A friend of mine once

164

rose up to admire the sunrise behind the blind just as four or five ducks came along. Another time a flock came over our blind from the *land* side. That particular blind had no roof on it, so there we were, crouched in plain view when we heard the whistling of their wings. Always when one of the blind's tenants is out in back answering a call of nature, ducks fly over. Always if you take out the boat to pick up one dead duck among the decoys, a flock of ten will come along while you are out there. Or a flock of ducks will splash into the decoys from goodness knows where, while you and your hunting companion are looking up and down the lake through the peepholes in the sides. Things like that.

On the other side of the coin, a friend of mine was sitting in the blind on my land about noon one warm day early in the season. It was a time of year, and of the day, when nobody in his right mind would expect to see a duck. All of a sudden he saw approaching a flock of some five hundred bluebills flying parallel to the shoreline.

He had not the faintest idea that they would decoy. Singles and doubles and triples decoy to join what they consider to be a larger flock. Obviously five hundred bluebill wouldn't turn in to join a dozen or so whistlers.

But they turned in and started to land. The air was full of ducks. Literally. My friend shot the three times you are allowed to shoot. The ducks flew on. And when he took a hasty look among the decoys he found he was in deep trouble.

He had shot and killed almost twice his limit. They were so thick that when you shot at one, you hit a lot of others next to and behind it.

Scared stiff, he left the ducks right where they were, ran up the bank and got into his car. He drove to the house where his wife was getting lunch. She grabbed her license and rode back with him.

Then and then only did he heave a sigh of relief and row out to get his ducks.

Some blinds are built over shallow water, on platforms held up by stakes driven into the mud of the bottom. You reach these only by boat. If there's a windstorm of any proportions you don't reach them at all. Or if the waves slosh up through the floorboards of the platform and the weather is freezing, maybe you wish you hadn't reached them. Because walking around on ice with a loaded gun in your hands makes going to war a safe occupation by comparison.

The later in the season it gets, the better the blind-hunting grows. And the colder you get waiting for the ducks. I'm used to being so cold and shivering so much that the gun barrel waves at the ducks. I'm used to having ice build up on the decoys until they tip over. I'm used to hand-warmers, thermal boots, overcoats over my overcoat—things like that. If my fingers don't turn white I consider it's been a warm day. It's half the fun to be able to complain bitterly about these conditions to fellow hunters and swap lies with them.

Hunting from a blind is likely to put meat on the table, but it is also likely to take up a lot of your time. Ducks fly the best just at dawn and just at dusk. So at the cottage I used to sit in the blind early and late. Then, if the wind wasn't too strong, I'd leave the decoys anchored out in front of the blind between times. Every half-hour or so during the working day I'd leave the typewriter for a careful peek over the bank to see if any live ducks were swimming around among the decoys. Mostly there weren't any—decoyed ducks are likely to leave when they get no response from the wooden ones—but a few times there were strangers there, and I took the shotgun and tried to sneak down where I could get a shot at them. I was never away from the desk more than five minutes, and very occasionally I'd return with dinner for two.

The unorthodox, but perfectly legal, ways of getting ducks are legion, and are mostly a closed book to those who, not needing the meat, aren't about to embrace the work entailed. Mostly the work entailed is a prodigious, unbelievable amount of walking, and an equally prodigious amount of crawling along on your stomach while you try to hide behind not much of anything. You can understand why anybody who has plenty of meat, or the money to buy it, is likely to look with a jaundiced eye on all that difficult walking and crawling. He wants to jeep there and back or he wants no part of it.

The walking and crawling bit is part of what is called "sneaking" ducks. Sneaking ducks is an undertaking which requires all the skills of a warpath Indian, combined with the abilities of a pro baseball pitcher. And this combination of talents is not easy to come by.

Briefly, you walk parallel to the lakeshore from one bay to the next. You'll find too that whatever Force situated the bays on Lake Champlain, put them pretty far apart. This is definitely a factor when you must look into each bay as you come to it without being seen by any ducks that are feeding in there.

The first time you try this you will look into a bay and find it empty. You'll then move confidently out into the open. And when you are in plain sight ducks will start popping out of water and taking flight; dozens of ducks. You'll be much too far away to shoot successfully and you will have blown a fine opportunity. The ducks had all been under the surface feeding when you first looked for them.

So you walk along to the next bay. We'll say that you find ducks there, and that you aren't seen by them when you peer out from behind some cedars to look. However, you're at one end of the bay and they're near the middle. There's no cover that you can see to help you get closer. The land slopes up away from the shore and it is pasture land.

It's up to you to use every tall thistle, bush, tuft of grass, old burdock, to get yourself to the water's edge unseen. You do this by counting while the ducks are all underwater, to establish the number of seconds you'll have between the time the last duck dives and the first duck pops out again. You'll have that much time—maybe a maximum of a minute, but don't count on it—to sprint to the next hiding place and throw yourself flat behind it.

What if there's *no* time between the last duck to go under and the first duck to come up? Then you'll have to crawl the whole distance on your belly, your shirtfront scooping in snow at the neck, your gun plugging, your hands like frozen hooks. And probably being seen about halfway there by some wise old drake whistler who suddenly notices a hump (that's you) up there in the pasture where there wasn't a hump yesterday. He'll take off and alert all the others.

But if their diving is fairly regular you can reach the edge of the bank in short sprints, can wait till all the ducks are under, and then sprint harder than ever for the water's edge. There you'll stand, panting with exertion and shaking with cold and excitement, your gun pointed at the place where the ducks went under.

You may get the first duck that pops out, maybe even two of them. The rest will be watching the bottoms of the first ones up, and after the surfaced ones get airborne, those others still in the lake will swim a vast distance *underwater*—sideways, out, every other way—and will come up flying. Most of them will come up out of range, because a duck can hold his breath an unbelievable length of time. You aren't likely to get one of those. They'll pop out at places and distances from you that seem impossible. One last one will always pop out minutes after you thought they'd all gone.

So now it will be up to you to retrieve your two ducks. Having gone through that much torture to get them, you aren't about to leave them there.

Of course if it isn't too late in the fall, you can wade or swim out to them after laying off as much or as little

168

clothing as the population of the area dictates. But you so seldom get anything but near-freezing air temperature during duck season, that you'll probably be confronted with ice along the water's edge, built up by freezing spray from the waves. You won't be about to risk double pneumonia even for two ducks.

This is where the skills of the professional baseball pitcher come in. You start throwing stones *beyond* each of your ducks so that the waves which the stones make will drive the ducks in toward shore a few inches each time.

I hasten to add that this too sounds a lot simpler than it is. If the ducks are far out, you obviously aren't going to be able to throw a very heavy stone clear out beyond them. If the wind is blowing out away from shore, and it mostly is because ducks pick sheltered bays to feed in, you've got to fire your rocks pretty rapidly even to keep ahead of the wind which is working against *you*. Also you've got to land the rocks fairly close to the ducks so that the waves when they reach the ducks will be big enough to do some good.

And so at some time during the operation (your skill dictating how often), you're going to *under*throw a rock. And when this happens you're going to undo the good that about three rocks have done. Because a thrown rock always makes much bigger waves in the direction in which it has been thrown, than it makes back toward shore.

But we'll say that you do make progress. You are able to throw bigger and bigger rocks as the ducks get closer to shore, and this speeds things up. The last ten feet or so can be covered in jig time by tossing huge boulders.

So you have your two ducks, and now you must walk back over the same distance you covered getting there. Nobody has to give you a sleeping pill that night.

Was it worth while?

Obviously from a sporting angle, in good times, no. But at the time Marg and I were married, when the Great Depression hung over the land, and when I was trying to learn my trade—boy, was it *ever* worth while! It was so worth while that two ducks called for a major celebration with maybe even candlelight. The rest of the dinner might consist of potatoes and canned string beans from the garden, hot homemade rolls and wild honey, a Waldorf salad with drop apples and hickory-nut meats, and for dessert—the celebration splurge—ice cream. The total cost would be under thirty cents for the ingredients in the rolls and for the ice cream itself. It would *have* to be that little. The particular editorial check that we were doling money from at the time would have to last until there was another check, which might be a heartbreaking length of time away.

Somehow the editorial checks did always manage to arrive in the nick of time, though. But not without help from us in stretching the previous ones, and in belt-tightening by hunting.

The closest call came when Margie, our daughter, was born. That was an expense that couldn't be put off or done without. Marg entered the hospital with no foggiest notion where the money for the doctor and hospital would come from. But while she was there *Love Story* magazine, a well-known pulp-paper all-fiction magazine of those years, bought and paid for a four-part serial. This took care of both hospital and doctor and left some besides. We used to say that after this check came, Margie was ours free and clear.

Unorthodox methods of getting ducks consist mostly of some variation on sneaking. Some of these methods are pretty ingenious and most of them have spur-of-the-moment improvisations made necessary by terrain and other conditions. One fall after we got a freezer, I worked every morning in front of a window from which I could see the far point, two and a half miles

170

away, and the whole north side of Owl's Head Bay. About once a morning, feeding ducks would swim around the point and toward me into the bay. I'd leave the desk and sneak up on them from behind some cedar trees on the bank. Mostly I'd get one or maybe even two. I had a boat up there so I didn't need to go through the rock-throwing routine. The whole operation might take half an hour. I'd conscientiously make up this lost writing time at the end of my working day. I figured that the time to get ducks was when they were gettable. If you had to work in the late afternoon to make up, you were still time and ducks ahead.

Unexpected things happened to you here too. Once I fired from under the branch of one of those cedars. I was in an awkward position with my head turned, bent a little forward, trying from this position to squint along the barrel. I fired and the gun's recoil caught me partly on the nose. I got a beautifully swelled nose in a deep, passionate purple from that one, with both eyes black and later a dirty yellow.

That fall we got quite a few ducks ahead in the freezer. And then we erased a lot of social debts by having a duck feed, with a whole duck per person (wild ducks are of course much smaller than tame ones). This was a real gourmet affair at less than hot-dog prices.

Once that same fall I drove over to Middlebury and was returning in the late afternoon. As I crossed the Hospital Creek bridge I saw a flock of black ducks circling to land in one of the creek's bays. I pulled over to the side of the road and watched them circle. They went down in back of a hill and didn't come up again.

I took Marg and the household supplies back to the cottage, grabbed my shotgun and boots, and drove right back down there. I left the car and began sneaking operations. I went 'way out around hills, and I followed gullies, and finally I crawled the last little way on my stomach, moving only while the ducks were underwater

171

feeding. For a change, everything was with me that day and I got close in for a shot. I got three ducks, and black ducks are the biggest ducks we have. This meant three meals for Marg and me (to say nothing about duck down for a pillow) because there was none of this one-duck-to-a-person when the ducks were black ducks. That's what I mean by improvising in the light of conditions, and of doing your hunting when the ducks were pretty obviously available. I wasn't away from the cottage much more than half an hour that time.

Marg hunted sometimes with me, mostly from a blind. Several times another couple and the Hoyts spent a Saturday morning together in the blind. Marg was pretty effective, too. The male hunters would try for three shots. They'd knock down ducks all over the place but they might end up getting none of them. Marg had a double-barreled 20-gauge shotgun. She would knock down a duck with the first shot, and instead of trying for another would stand there with her gun pointed at the one she'd downed. If it so much as twitched a feather she would let it have the other barrel.

Another variation on the sneaking, was a framework for the front of the canoe and into which we'd woven cedars. When that framework was set over the bow and the canoe was coming toward you, it looked like a clump of bushes; you couldn't see any part of the canoe, even the paddle.

As I've said, the ducks would sit out in the middle of the lake all day sleeping. This was a maddening set-up to a person on shore scraping the bottom of the larder: all those fine meals just sitting out there, completely unattainable.

So after work, when there was little or no wind, I'd now and then launch the clump of bushes with the canoe nestled behind them and start for a raft of ducks toward the middle of the lake.

I'd paddle quite fast during the early part of the trip, but when I got partway there I'd slow down and paddle without removing the blade from the water. As I got still nearer I'd slow down even more, until there was little or no wake. To the ducks, I must have looked like a small island which grew slightly larger each time they looked toward it. But there was no sign of a person or a movement; my canoe-blind did not seem to be moving.

There would come a time, however, no matter how careful I was, when certain ducks would begin to show signs of nervousness. They'd stretch their necks high, quack, begin to swim tentatively away. You watched them through the cedars very carefully. When the first ones had all the ducks moving away, were even showing signs of flight, the showdown time had come.

You very slowly and carefully removed the paddle from the water, picked up the gun, planted your feet so you wouldn't tip the whole shebang over, rose up, and fired.

Sometimes you'd get a duck, sometimes you wouldn't. I don't think I ever got more than one to pay for the slow, laborious trip out there. And if you didn't get one, the trip back to the cottage seemed even longer than the trip out had been. On the way out you were buoyed by excitement and anticipation. On the way back, empty-handed, you just paddled.

Sometimes the larder would be in such a precarious condition that we'd shoot mergansers—fish ducks. These ducks have an incredibly bad image when it comes to eatability. They smell and taste like fish, which is the staple of their diet. And more fish we did not need. Fish secondhand, so to speak, robs it of all its delicacy and leaves nothing but the obnoxious qualities, isolated and many times magnified, to slap you in the palate.

We probably would never even have tried mergansers if Harry Irwin, a friend of ours, had not passed on to us a method of preparing them which made them edible, even enjoyable. I wouldn't eat them in preference to any other duck, ever. But if I didn't have any other duck, I would, and did, eat them.

You cut the two breast pieces away from the rest of the carcass. You may or may not want to use a clothespin over your nose while you do this. You lay these slabs of flesh on a plate and cover them with a thick layer of salt. Both sides. You leave them that way for three days. You add more salt if the original melts and becomes brine. Pour off the brine before you add more.

At the end of three days wash the salt off in a couple of waters and broil or fry the two slabs of meat. The fish odor and taste will be gone, and the meat will taste more like filet mignon than it does like duck. Not enough so you'll go around shooting nothing but mergansers, but passable.

When you prepare any of Lake Champlain's ducks for the table you should soak them overnight in as heavy a brine as you can make. Be sure the whole duck is covered. This will draw the blood. Wash them off and roast them. Stuffing the carcass with dressing is a delightful extra.

Ducks are in bountiful supply in the fall on Lake Champlain or any other large lake along one of their flyways. But being in bountiful supply and being easy to get are two distinctly different things.

Your success is not measured by your blood-dripping sadistic will to kill, as hunting critics seem to assume. Very simply, your success is measured by how hungry you are.

Because it's in direct ratio to how hungry you are that you will consider it worth the while to spend those countless hours in a blind, and suffer stoically the incredible tortures of sneaking that would make an Indian fakir on a bed of nails sigh in comfort by comparison.

In short, you've got to want or need duck very badly. And believe me, I did. But having said that, I'll admit there are two intangibles to duck-hunting that are terrific plusses.

174

First there are the moments of incredibly high excitement, which breed absorption and interest. And second there is the primitive instinct to bring home food for the mate and young which lies dormant in all of us. This brings you a feeling of pride in your success that is most rewarding; you've provided for your family with your own hands.

With those things added to meat-on-the-table, how basic can you get?

14

What—A Turkey Hunt in a Vermont Barn?

Ducks were the game most often available to us. But there were other meats, too, that came to us through hunting. I even hunted deer a few times, but I was always a lousy deer-hunter. However, in Vermont, at the time we were living at the cottage, rabbits were legal game even in the summer, so we'd start out after work with shotguns, and head for several acres of newly cleared land which had brushpiles. We'd make the rounds of the brushpiles. One of us would climb up on the first pile; then he'd leap straight up and come down in the middle of it, hard. He'd repeat the leap three or four times on each pile.

Rabbits like to hide in brushpiles during the day. Maybe we'd draw a blank on the first couple of piles. But usually from one of them a rabbit would explode out and away from the sheltering brush. If we were agile, and a good enough shot, we'd eat rabbit that night. And rabbit is delicious, and tastes like chicken. It's well to soak the dressed carcass of a rabbit in brine just as you do a duck's. But if you're in a hurry and need the meat that night, soaking it a couple of hours is enough.

Another method of getting rabbits, one which Sid Gage and I turned to often when he was visiting us, was to drive slowly along 'way-back country roads with one of us lying out on the front fender with the shotgun in position to fire forward. Rabbits take to the roads in the early morning after a heavy dew. In that way they keep out of the tall wet grass. When you come up on them slowly, they'll mostly run along the road ahead of you, loath to leap into that wet grass. This can be their undoing. Sid was very fond of rabbit pie, and this stratagem furnished us many a rabbit pie.

You couldn't use this method today. Laws have been passed which make it illegal to carry a loaded gun in a car, to shoot from a right-of-way; and rightly so. But when we did it there were more deserted back roads, less people, less cars. In the years we did this, only once did we ever meet another car or see a person. Besides, today the cars are so streamlined that there would be no place for the gunner to stretch out. And above all there would be no runningboard for him to rest his toes on.

Pheasants in our section of Vermont are practically non-existent now. But they were fairly plentiful when we were feeding ourselves from Nature at the cottage. You were allowed to shoot the male birds on Wednesdays and Saturdays during the season. We ate a lot of pheasants. And even though we didn't serve them under glass, they were plenty delicious and a regular gourmet item.

One October morning when we were sleeping on the cottage porch I woke about daylight and saw a couple of pheasants moving along the line of cedars at the edge of our cliff. They were moving from south to north, and would pass about twenty-five feet from where we were lying there in bed.

I very carefully rolled out on the far side, bent double and hidden by the bed. Still bent over, I opened the door into the living room, moved through it.

Once out of sight I straightened up, jumped for the gun, grabbed and loaded it. I slid through the door into the kitchen. I moved through the kitchen and out the back door. It was very cold and, as a newlywed, I was not extensively bundled up. The north wind greeted me as I opened the back door. Talk about its whistling through the bare branches: it sure whistled through my bare branches. Everything I walked on was incredibly cold to my bare feet.

I moved to the corner of the house. I stuck the side of my face and one eye out around it to see where the pheasants were. They hadn't got there yet. I waited, shivering.

Suddenly the cock pheasant walked into view. I stepped out into sight, then fired. The bird dropped and I ran to get him, colder than ever, but triumphant. I left him on the back porch for attention later and, with chattering teeth, went back to bed to get warm.

Partridge we got occasionally. But we had no dog, and a partridge can explode from close under your feet, if you have no warning from a dog that he's there, in a way that will cause your nervous system to go all to pieces. By the time you get your heart back down out of your mouth and turn around (partridges much prefer to explode in back of you to make the effect more devastating), the bird will have swooped behind the nearest tree and be keeping it nicely between you and him. So we didn't get a lot of partridges.

Once when I was hunting in prickly-ash clumps for rabbits or partridges, that first summer after we were married, I started around a clump one way with plenty of noise, then sneaked around the other way quietly. I came face to face with what I thought was a partridge. It flew, I shot, it went down.

When I came to it, to my horror it had long tail-feathers—which a partridge doesn't have. It was a hen pheasant. They look about the same except for the tail-feathers. But partridges were in season and hen pheasants never were legal.

Well, the bird was dead. I wouldn't have shot it if I hadn't been mistaken in my identification. But I couldn't bring it back to life. I saw no sense in wasting a fine bird. On the other hand I wasn't about to be fined for possessing illegal game.

I quickly shoved the carcass into the edge of a prickly-ash clump, covered it with leaves and went on hunting. Under the guise of searching for game, I assured myself there was nobody around. I was close to the lake on one side so it was easier to do this than it would otherwise have been. That cut in half the area I had to search. Then I walked on home to the cottage, hunting as I went.

Late in the afternoon I took the canoe and paddled down the lake to the pasture where the prickly-ash clumps were located. I searched the area with my eyes carefully as I paddled. I saw nobody.

I landed and walked to the clumps I had been hunting when the hen pheasant and I had had our accident. I began to look around. That clump over there must be the one, yet it didn't look just right.

I searched; there was no pile of leaves, no pheasant. I tried the next clump. That one looked right, but there was no bird hidden there either. The next looked perfect except for one thing. You guessed it: there was no bird.

I then realized something that I had never noticed before. Every prickly-ash clump in a pasture looks about like every other prickly-ash clump in that pasture. The more clumps there are, and the closer together they are, the truer this is.

I began to get panicky. All sorts of ideas went through my guilty mind. Had somebody seen me hide the

178

bird, and was he waiting for my return? No, because if that were so he would have left the bird there and pounced on me when I retrieved it. Maybe somebody had seen me, wanted the bird, and had taken it after I left. Or maybe the bird had come to life and flown away, scattering the leaves.

All the while I kept looking. I tried every sort of recognition stratagem, all to no avail. It began to get dark. I searched on.

Finally, just as it was getting good and dark, my eye was attracted to a pile of leaves next to a clump of ash that looked nothing whatever like the clump where I had hidden the bird. I kicked at the leaves. And there was the bird.

I took it to the canoe and paddled back to the cottage. In my heart I wondered, as I paddled, if that long and traumatic search hadn't been my punishment for shooting a hen pheasant. I probably ought to add that the bird tasted bitter, to further my punishment. But it didn't taste bitter. It tasted simply delicious.

There was one other bit of hunting that didn't net me food. But this was the most amazing hunt I was ever on. It was a turkey-hunt in a part of Vermont where, at that time, there were no wild turkeys.

Bill Burpee's family had given up the farm near Dead Creek and moved to a farm on Route 22-A just south of Addison. They had a flock of turkeys that had been allowed to run free all summer, and when the family came to move they couldn't catch the turkeys to move them too. So Bill organized some of his friends to help.

The turkeys roosted in the hay barn at night, and Bill drove down there well after dark and shut the main doors. Then in the morning we all gathered to begin the simple task of taking them into custody and bagging them for the short journey to their new home.

It became apparent immediately that the turkeys took a dim view of Project Custody. And that they had no intention of going quietly. In fact—let's face it—they had no intention of going at all. With much gobbling and fuss and feathers, some of them flew at once to the barn's big crossbeams from the floor of the drive-in unloading area between the two mows. When we arrived they had been eating grain off that floor, thoughtfully provided by Bill.

We charged a couple of the ones that remained on the barn floor. They squawked, eluded us, and joined the ones already peering down from the big wide beams.

We tried driving others into a corner, two-on-one, and we got a few. But pretty soon we were faced with all the remaining turkeys peering down from those big beams while we looked up from below.

The mows on each side were about half full of hay. From the sloping edge of the hay in the mow you couldn't quite reach the crossbeams, but you almost could. So, after considerable figuring, we all climbed up into the mows. From the edge of the hay Bill picked out a husky bird, then launched himself up in the air toward it.

He grabbed its feet expertly with one hand. And with the bird squawking and flapping above him like an animated parachute, he landed on the side of the mow and slid the rest of the way down the hay to the barn floor.

I immediately picked out a bird, jumped for it, grabbed its legs. And, with my flopping parachute, slid down the side of the mow to the barn floor. The other guys followed suit. You had to slide; you couldn't stop yourself once you had jumped.

In the meantime Bill had bagged his bird and tied the mouth of the gunnysack. He was on his way back up into the mow while I bagged mine.

That began one of the most hilarious episodes of my life. The birds soon learned to take evasive action. But they couldn't stay in the air long, and if they landed in the mow there were a lot of us there to charge them.

180

Sooner or later they'd end up on the crossbeams. Immediately, from the edge of the mow, a human projectile would launch itself, grab a pair of legs (or sometimes just one—and in that case *what* flapping and squawking!), and would slide down the front of the mow with the turkey held triumphantly aloft.

Sometimes you'd miss the legs and slide the rest of the way without a bird. Gradually we got all but one. He had seen the door open when someone carried a captured bird outside, and he had veered through the opening to freedom. He was the only one, though, that wasn't captured, bagged, and later released in a brand-new wire enclosure at the new farm.

What happened to him? We gathered with Bill the next Saturday to hunt him down with shotguns because he was avoiding the barn like the plague and living in a small patch of woods near by, roosting in a tree. Winter was coming on, when he'd freeze or starve. We drove the woods, and he'd fly to the other end. We'd drive back, and he'd fly to where he had been before. We finally gave up. I never heard what finally became of him; I think Bill probably got him. But that ended my one and only turkey-hunt. And if you could have seen people jumping out, then sliding down the mow with a huge bird by the legs, I think you would agree with me that it was one of the most unusual turkey-hunts ever held.

So there are hunters and hunters. And maybe this will explain some of us little-guy, meat-on-the-table hunters. We're just trying to get along. In my case, at the cottage, hunting was one of the things which helped pull me through the earlier stages of trying to learn my profession.

15

Then and Now

When my parents built the cottage it was very
primitive. It was really a camp. And it was very lovely. It
had a panoramic, an amazing, view of the lake and
mountains. It had privacy in the extreme. It had clean
air, clean water. The area was rural, a land of working
farms.

As the years rolled by there were changes. They
came slowly, almost imperceptibly. The first change was
from horses to cars.

During the earliest years we were there, if we wanted
to go to Vergennes or Middlebury my father would get
up very early and walk the two miles to the farm. He
would take a halter and go out into the pasture to get
Pony, the Morgan horse I mentioned earlier.

Invariably Pony was not buying this routine. She
would remain with her head down, eating, until my
father got within a few feet of her. Then she would toss
her head, kick up her heels, and gallop to the far corner
of the pasture. My father would go after her at a more
sedate pace.

She would remain eating until the last moment, then
gallop back where she had been before. If my father tried
to corner her against the fence she would start one way to
make him start in that direction. Then she would gallop
triumphantly in the other direction like a basketball
player head-faking his opponent.

My father would grow grimmer, more unhappy,
more determined, with each try. Pony kept the game

alive by making it seem as if he *almost* caught her each time. He just couldn't believe that on the next try he wouldn't be successful.

But the time available would be fleeting, and sooner or later he would give up. He would go in and get a measure of oats and approach Pony, the measure held out in one hand and the halter behind him in the other.

This changed the game completely. The idea now was to get the oats without letting the halter be put over her head. Pony was a past master at the game.

Of course the easiest thing was to knock the measure out of my father's hand, and then come back for the spilled oats later. But my father had learned this maneuver and held the measure very tightly. Pony still did pretty well. She'd get a mouthful or two of oats and get away scot-free most of the time. Occasionally, though, my father would win this phase of the game—enough times to keep him playing.

However, mostly Pony would win. Time would continue to pass and my father would get desperate. He would go to the house and call his mother, my grandmother.

She was a wispy little lady and she always wore black dresses, very full, which swept the ground and showed only the toes of her black shoes.

She would march out to the pasture, spurning the halter and the measure of oats.

She would say very sternly, "Pony, you come here this instant."

Pony would stop eating, walk over, nuzzle my grandmother fondly. She'd hold her head down so Grandmother could reach her easily, and allow herself to be led to the barn by the mane. My father would stand watching this, gnashing his teeth.

He would then harness Pony, drive up to the cottage, load the rest of the party, and start out.

At that time there were already a few cars on the

road. These would frighten horses—particularly Pony when she wasn't tired—scatter and kill hens and chickens, make life hideous for one and all with their noise and the clouds of dust they stirred up. Some of them would tear around at speeds as high as *fifteen* miles an hour.

Of course they didn't always travel at such breakneck speed. In the earliest days of cars, at least one area of Vermont had a law which required that anyone driving an automobile be preceded on foot by a grown man carrying a red flag.

Even in my time I can remember a sign where the Potash Bay road dropped down into a gully. It read: CAUTION. AUTOMOBILES MUST NOT TRAVEL MORE THAN 6 MILES PER HOUR. BY ORDER OF THE SELECTMEN. The sign remained there for years, growing more dilapidated and harder to read; nobody bothered to take it down. Bushes grew up in front of it until cars whizzing by at fifty miles an hour couldn't even see it.

As time went by more cars appeared. Horses, cattle, men, and even poultry to a limited degree, got used to them. My father never owned a car, but still they affected our life at the cottage. People took us places in cars, came to visit us in cars, and we hired cars now and then.

At first everything in our area was carried from place to place by teams of horses hitched to wagons of various kinds. I've mentioned the hayracks; these could be taken off the narrow body of the wagon, which could then be used for hauling manure or gravel.

Gradually these teams and wagons gave way to trucks on the road. And on the farm land, the teams gave way to tractors. The first ones had iron wheels and the later ones had rubber tires.

To take care of these new vehicles the roads changed. When travel was strictly by wagon the roads got pretty messy after a rain. Addison County is blessed —or cursed, depending on your point of view—with clay

185

soil. If not handled right, this cracks in the droughts of summer. The saying used to be, "I lost three cows down one of those cracks."

But drought times really weren't the problem. It was during rainy times that you got into real difficulty. You see, the same clay which would crack when it was dry, would cling to things when it was wet. Your feet would become about three times normal size. In really wet places, you'd sink to your ankles. It would get on your clothes and hands if you worked in it long. It would glob up anything and everything. And it was bottomless. A team and wagon traveling (or trying to) down the middle of the road would leave unbelievable ruts.

And if it was bad for teams, it was impossible for cars. Addison County clay had all the characteristics of a high-grade lubricating grease when it was wet. The narrow tires of the early cars just spun and burrowed deeper and deeper into the slime. You couldn't jack the car up to put chains on because the jack and anything under it would simply be forced down into the mud. Certain farmers with an unusually muddy area in front of their houses were accused of taking water out to their mudholes when they started to dry up so as to continue the cash income their teams were earning by pulling cars out of the mud. John Godfrey Saxe, a poet, eulogized this clay for young lovers who wanted to ride out in a sleigh on a Sunday afternoon in spring when part of the snow had melted and part of the road was bare. They had no problem, he said, if they stuck to clay roads, because the runners of the sleigh would travel over the wet clay even more easily than over the snow.

As the number of cars increased, such conditions just weren't tolerated by the taxpayers. The remedy was to gravel the road. You "crowned them up" for good drainage—mounded them with a "road machine" by making a ditch on each side—and graveled the crown. Cars could travel over these graveled roads wet or dry.

But this presented another problem: washboard. With heavy travel in dry weather, the surface would become corrugated. It looked just like the old-fashioned washboard. And you had to know how to drive on washboard or else you'd be shaken loose from your teeth.

If you traveled slowly, you'd bounce. If you traveled fast, you and the car would be shaken to pieces—you figuratively, the car literally.

But there was a speed between thirty-five and forty miles an hour which would allow you to hit the corrugations just right. And Presto!—you would ride along smoothly and easily.

Again, as the number of cars increased, the taxpayers rebelled. The answer was hard-surface roads. All this took many, many years. But it all affected us at the cottage in little ways.

For one thing, our mail used to be delivered by an R.F.D. mailman riding behind a horse in a sort of outhouse on wheels, painted red, white and blue, and lettered U.S. MAIL. Then one historic day he came in an automobile. And he has continued to come that way ever since. The auto was nowhere near as fancy, but it got around the route faster. We found that it became easier to get other things besides mail delivered to us, too.

When I first remember the farms near us, they each had a "lake pasture." The fences outlining such a pasture were extended into the lake with long poles set horizontally into the V's formed by crossed short poles driven into the mud. They were extended out far enough so the cows would have to swim to get around them. Most cows were loath to do this. But there were always a few hardy non-conformists that would swim around these fences and then wander off through gardens, cornfield, meadows and yards—anywhere there was lush eating. This happened most often when the farmer had been very busy in haying, the water had gone down in the lake the way it does all summer, and the fence needed a

187

new section added. The farmer would swear mightily as he collected his cows and fixed his water-fence.

On hot days in summer the cows would spend the middle of each day out in the water where the flies couldn't get at their legs and bellies, and where their tails could flick cool water when they flicked flies. Naturally the mud would get churned up by their wading out; nor were they always fastidious. The current carried this mess along.

Because the cows got around the water-fences so often, or because people complained, or both, the farmers fenced off the lakeshore as soon as the electric motor came along and water could be pumped to a pasture trough automatically. Today there are comparatively few water-fences. This gradual change was a boon to us: we no longer had a mess to contend with when the wind and current were wrong for us.

Our cottage went from hand-pumped water to a pressure tank filled automatically to give us running water. The original hand-pump grew temperamental and decrepit, so for several years before the automatic system was installed we carried water from the lake in twelve-quart pails. Farms that had access to the lake followed the same course. The only difference was that we took up our suction line in the winter, and they buried theirs to avoid freezing. Farms that were away from the lake used cisterns and wells—mostly wells—as a source of supply.

But in more recent times Addison experienced extended droughts two summers in a row. Farmers had to put aside much of their other work and draw or pump water from the lake or creeks to keep their cows alive and their milk production up. To a farmer five to ten miles from water, with his well dry, drawing enough water for one hundred head of cattle and his household needs presented a well-nigh impossible problem.

As a result of this situation, Senator George Aiken petitioned the proper authorities in the United States

188

government to build a water system comparable to a city system, using Lake Champlain as a source of supply. It would service the rural towns of Bridport, Shoreham and both Addisons, West and East.

The petition was approved and funded, and thus the Tri-Town Water System was born. It not only furnishes water and plenty of it, it furnishes good water. It filters, chlorinates, fluoridates, and has a back-up system in case of mechanical failure. This is a far cry from the hand-pumps, the cisterns, the wells of an earlier time.

Just as the old water-fences have mostly disappeared, gradually the older types of woven wire and barbed wire have given way to electric fences. This happens especially with temporary barriers designed to hold cattle in an unfenced meadow after the hay has been cut and more feed is needed than the regular pasture affords. One wire and even the thinnest sort of posts will suffice. Once a cow has taken a charge of current she isn't going near that fence again till she forgets. And she doesn't forget quickly. If the current is drawn from the farm buildings, and not provided by a battery, it will knock even a bull to his knees.

They had a low electric fence at the farm once, to hold in a number of pigs. The hens could pass under this without touching it at all, and only the rooster's tail-feathers touched. This he did not feel.

But there came a rainy day. And with his tail-feathers sopping wet, that handsome, arrogant rooster walked under the fence. His tail touched. There was a loud, outraged squawk, the rooster shot about five feet into the air. He lit running and he kept on squawking for a considerable while.

All summer this went on. He'd forget and feed under the fence; nothing would happen. He'd do it again and again; still nothing. But sometime there would come a rainy day, his wet tail-feathers would conduct the charge of electricity down into his rear end. Then would come

189

the heartfelt squawk, the convulsive leap high in the air, the continued poultry-type swearing for some time afterward. It *made* the summer for the farmer.

Actually, over those same years the farms went from big flocks of poultry to no poultry at all. You can drive all around Addison and West Addison today and not see a hen or a chicken out walking around. Specialists can raise hens and chickens cheaper than the dairy farmer can, so he specializes in milk and buys his eggs and chickens in the chain store. In Salisbury, Maple Meadows Farm has one building which is a regular egg factory. It produces about 10,000 eggs a day. The eggs are collected automatically; the hens fed and watered, their droppings carried away, all automatically.

In the same way, as I mentioned much earlier, machinery has caused the old haystack to disappear from the fields. Hay is field-bailed now, or cut and chopped and blown into a silo. The showpiece of the silo world is the big, blue, glass-lined Harvestore silo which you see as you drive around the countryside. It costs as much as a whole farm formerly cost.

The boats which used to come to Loomis's dock and unload knocked-down parts for apple boxes and later load boxes and barrels of apples, no longer come. They've disappeared from the lake, victims of the Depression and later of the cars and the planes. There used to be three of the boats, the *Vermont*, the *Ticonderoga* (which you can still see at Shelburne Museum) and the *Chataguay*. No big passenger boats ply the lake now.

Instead of wooden boxes or barrels the orchard uses cardboard cartons. They are brought there by huge trailer trucks, which carry away the apples.

Other boats that have disappeared are the tugs with their long strings of barges. These used to carry miscellaneous merchandise. The barges were mostly owned by the families who ran them. Sometimes, though, these families ran them for moneyed owners. There was a house toward the back of each barge in which the family lived. You'd paddle or row out to see a tow go past and you'd hear phonographs playing, see a lot of kids clambering around, see a large washing hanging out aboard each barge.

The barges used to be pulled two abreast. If you saw a tow broadside from the cottage and you could count ten barges, that meant there were actually nineteen or twenty of them.

Every year a barge used to come into the corner of Potash Bay (about half a mile from us) sometime during the summer to load bailed hay. The hayracks would pull up along the road at the edge of the cliff and unload into a chute which would slide the bales of hay down into the barge's hold. We used to go over and watch the hay being loaded.

When the barge came there, it would cut loose from a northbound tow and come into Potash Bay by hoisting a dirty old sail. When it was full and ready to head back for New York City, it would wait until it saw a southbound tow 'way up by Split Rock Mountain, and would hoist its sail again. It would go out to the middle of the lake and the tow would pick it up there. To help the sail and to steer, they used a huge sculling oar.

There was a very long tow-rope between the tug and the tows. My father used to tell about a number of incidents over the years where men had been returning home to Vermont at night, alone in a rowboat, drunk, back when Addison was dry and Port Henry wet. A man's judgment in such a case being less than perfect, he would not want to wait until the whole long tow passed, and would try to row under the tow-rope. The rope would slack a little, come tight once more, and flip the boat. The man would never be heard of again. His boat would be found floating upside down, the marks of the rope on it.

The place of these tows has been taken by the oil

barges, some of which are so large that they fill a whole lock in the canal. And the lowly rowboat has gone too, the victim of the outboard motor. The canoe, however, is alive and well and living on Lake Champlain.

When I was a small boy at the cottage the blast furnace at Port Henry would pour off its molten slag into the lake. This was spectacular any time, but at night it would light up everything for miles around for a few minutes when the act was performed. You could read a newspaper clear over at our cottage.

The blast furnace is closed down now, and has been for a long while. It's pollution would not be tolerated today, anyway. But I remember it as a most amazing experience to have the world all of a sudden light up with a fearful rumble.

The slag itself used to cool into gray pieces of rock, honeycombed, which would float. You could find these many miles away from the furnace. Even today you very occasionally pick up a piece of this slag left over from other times. You can astonish anyone by telling him the rock you are holding will float. And then by proving it.

When there was only one cottage between ours and Chimney Point, a group of elm trees near Oven Point used to be called the "Eagle Trees." Eagles used to bring their fish to the high branches, eat them there and digest them. We used to go there once or twice a summer to look for eagle plumes. I still have one of the plumes we found. Today the area is built up; the elms are mostly gone, and the eagles with them.

I have mentioned taking the ferry across Lake Champlain. There is no ferry at Chimney Point now. The Champlain Bridge was officially opened there in 1929 while I was in residence at the cottage, and I went down by canoe to watch the ceremonies from the water.

Obviously I had no way of knowing then that I would later marry the daughter of the man who had

192

checked the plans and ordered the material for the central span of that bridge.

The cottage now has its own phone, and a dial phone at that—shades of the old wall-box with the mouthpiece sticking out and the receiver hanging on its side! The icebox has long since been replaced by an electric refrigerator. The woodshed has become only a woodshed again, and we have a bathroom upstairs in the cottage. Our old cooking range gave way to a kerosene stove, which in turn gave way to a gas stove.

And we have electricity. No more kerosene lamps, no more candles (except when the current fails).

The summer that the electricity came to us—ah, that was a summer. I was married by then. We had the cottage wired, but we didn't say anything to the old-timers like Sid Gage, who had known the cottage from its earliest days.

Sid was to arrive with his wife about a week later. We planned carefully. We put the kerosene lamps on the shelf where they had always spent the daylight hours. That evening we lit one of them, placed it on the table and began to read by it. About nine o'clock the Gages arrived from Worcester. They came in; we talked.

At bedtime, Sid went to the lamp shelf and lit himself a lamp just as he always had. He and Marion started for the stairs. I sidled over to the switches and suddenly the place burst into light. I turned on everything within reach.

Sid's face was a study. But instead of looking happy, I thought he might be going to cry. And then, darned if I wasn't afraid I was going to cry myself.

Because an era was gone.

Don't get me wrong: every one of the conveniences, the improvements, we wanted and we welcomed. The cars, the roads, the phone, that electricity, the other things, we wouldn't have gone without.

But *all together,* that was something else. All together, that night, we knew vaguely that they had taken
something away from us. The primitive place with its
solitude, was gone. It was still a lovely place, but it was
different. And Sid and I knew it, and that night it had left
a big hole in each of us.

Sometimes things work out differently from the way
you expect them to work out. And our showing off our
new electricity to the Gages was one of these. But all in
all we have had a wonderful time at the cottage through
the years. No one can take from any of us the memories
of all the things that happened in that quiet place with its
beautiful surroundings.

194